WILLIAMSON'S *KIDS CAN!*®

REAL-WORLD MATH
for Hands-on Fun!

I only have $5, but you have 3800 Lire!

CINDY A. LITTLEFIELD

Illustrations by Michael Kline

WILLIAMSON PUBLISHING ■ CHARLOTTE, VERMONT

LIBRARY OF CONGRESS CATALOGING-IN-PUBLICATION DATA

Littlefield, Cynthia, 1956-
    Real-world math for hands-on fun! / Cynthia Littlefield ; illustrations by Michael Kline.
       p. cm. — (A Williamson kids can! book)
    Includes index.
    ISBN 1-885593-51-1 (pbk.)
    1. Mathematics—Study and teaching (Elementary) 2. Mathematics—Study and
teaching—Activity programs.   I. Kline, Michael P. II. Title
    QA135.5 .L548 2001
    510—dc21   2001017698

KIDS CAN!® SERIES EDITOR: **Susan Williamson**

PROJECT EDITOR: **Dana Pierson**

ILLUSTRATIONS: **Michael Kline**

INTERIOR DESIGN: **Bonnie Atwater**

COVER DESIGN: **Trezzo-Braren Studio**

PRINTING: **Capital City Press**

WILLIAMSON PUBLISHING CO.
P.O. Box 185 Charlotte, VT 05445   (800) 234-8791

Manufactured in the United States of America

10 9 8 7 6 5 4 3

CONTENTS

DEDICATION

To my kids, Ian and Jade, who continually remind me how much fun it is to learn something new. And to Kevin, who is always willing to lend a hand with each new endeavor.

ACKNOWLEDGMENTS

Thanks to Deanna Cook for her generosity and advice, and for being such an inspiration; thanks also to Adrienne Stolarz for enthusiastically helping me track down so many fun facts.

Discover the Real World of Math

Has an ostrich ever passed your parents' car on the way to the grocery store? Probably not, but the truth is that this long-legged bird can truck along at a speedy 40 miles (64 km) per hour! If that sounds amazing, think of this: During its lifetime, a gray whale migrates some 500,000 miles (800,000 km) — that's like swimming to the moon and back! If it weren't for math, we wouldn't be able to make such cool comparisons. Numbers give us a way to size up everything around us, from the distance a football player has to run to score a touchdown to how many ounces are in your bottle of soda.

Measuring is just one way we put numbers to use in our everyday lives. We also arrange them into codes when we program our CD player or VCR. And we rely on them to keep everything on schedule — think of all those planes, trains, and buses that take worldwide travelers where they want to go! In a way, you could say that math is like air. It's everywhere — in the kitchen when you bake brownies, at a carnival when you buy a raffle ticket, even on the weather station when meteorologists track a spiraling tropical storm.

That's what this book is all about — all the cool things you can do with math. You'll discover why triangles are used to build bridges and roofs, find one-of-a-kind symmetrical designs in the natural world, and learn how to make a million dollars in a month! So get ready to have a mathematically marvelous time!

NUMBERS:
THE GLOBAL LANGUAGE

8 LEGS

One, uno, un, yi, en. You may use one of these words depending on where you live, but they all mean the same thing: the number 1! Numbers are the words of a second language — mathematics — that's spoken everywhere!

Every day in Canada, Spain, France, Brazil, China, and Kenya, or any other country you can think of, people use numbers in all kinds of ways. Carpenters use them to build things; chefs use them to prepare delicious foods; athletes use them to keep score; doctors use them to prescribe medicines; pilots use them to fly at certain altitudes; and scientists use them to measure everything from the height of a mountain to the strength of an earthquake.

Numbers can be lots of fun, and they turn up in some surprising places — even in the middle of an apple! Read on to discover ways that number sequences, patterns, and codes "talk" to all of us, no matter what other languages we speak.

If you traveled back in time, you might not recognize those dashing *digits* (another word for numbers) we know as 1 to 10.

MAYAN-STYLE MATH!

The Mayans of ancient Mexico used a number system based on increments (increases) of 20. This is different from the American custom of using English units, which are based on the number 10. The figures for zero through 19 in Mayan, however, are very easy to understand. They are written with only three symbols:

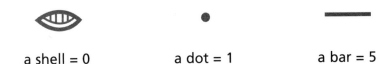

a shell = 0   a dot = 1   a bar = 5

0	1	2	3
5	6	7	8
10	11	12	13

Here's what the numbers zero through 19 looked like in Mayan:

Try using these numbers to do some simple arithmetic. Can you solve the following problems? Write your answers in Mayan numbers, of course, on a sheet of paper! Check your results with the answers on the next page.

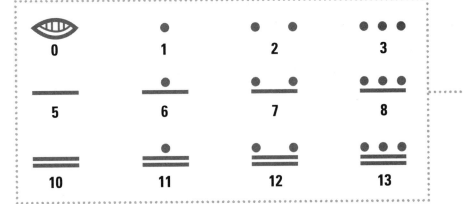

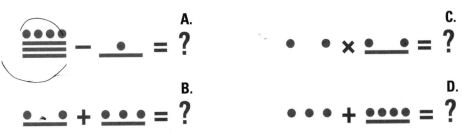

Decoding Other Languages

Sometimes, the *prefix* of a word (the letters before the main word) can give us a clue to its meaning. Look at the following Latin and Greek words whose prefixes appear in the English words at right.

uni = one

duo = two

tri = three

quattuor = four

quinque = five

sex = six

septem = seven

octo = eight

novem = nine

deca = ten

Mayan-Style Math: A. 13; B. 15; C. 14; D. 12.

13	15	14	12

A Number by Another Name

All of the words on the left are based on a particular number from 1 to 10. On a separate sheet of paper (please don't write in your book), see if you can match them up with the correct meanings. (When you're done, compare your answers with the ones at the bottom of the page.)

1.	Sextuplets	A.	A two-family house
2.	Septuagenarian	B.	Ninth month in the early Roman calendar
3.	Decade	C.	Ocean animal with eight arms
4.	Tricuspid	D.	Group of five singers or musicians
5.	Quintet	E.	Six children born together
6.	Octopus	F.	Ten years
7.	Unicycle	G.	A tooth with three cusps
8.	Duplex	H.	A vehicle with one wheel
9.	November	I.	A verse with four lines
10.	Quatrain	J.	A person in his 70s

During the day, listen to conversations around your home or school. Can you come up with other words that begin in the same ways as the ones listed here? How about *unicorn, tricycle, octagon, triathlete,* and *uniform*?

CHING CHING!

A Number by Another Name: 1. E; 2. J; 3. F; 4. G; 5. D; 6. C; 7. H; 8. A; 9. B; 10. I.

WRITE LIKE A ROMAN

When the ancient Romans numbered things — such as the doors in the Colosseum — they used letters as numbers. But you don't need to go to Italy to see *Roman numerals*. You can often spot them etched in stone on the front of an old building or on a clock or watch. Here's all you need to know to read them:

I = 1   C = 100
V = 5   D = 500
X = 10   M = 1000
L = 50

♦ If a larger numeral follows a smaller one, subtract the first from the second.

IV means: V – I (or 5 – 1 = 4)

♦ If a numeral is followed by one or more symbols that are equal to or less than it, add them together.

XIII means: X + I + I + I (or 10 + 1 + 1 + 1 = 13)

♦ When you're writing a number like the year 1999, the thousands, hundreds, tens, and ones columns are represented individually.

1,000	+	900	+	90	+	9
M	+	CM	+	XC	+	IX
(1,000)		(1,000 – 100 = 900)		(100 –10 = 90)		(10 –1 = 9)

1999 = M CM XC IX

(Usually this is written MCMXCIX, which is certainly a little more difficult to decipher.)

Well, Claudius... I'll just have to go with door number III!

☆ **When were you born?**

Now that you know how it's done, write the year of your birth, remembering to separate each number.

Make a Match!

Here's a fun game you and a friend can play that poses two (make that II!) challenges — matching up Roman numerals and Arabic numbers (the ones we use every day), and remembering where you saw them last!

On separate index cards, use Arabic numbers to write:

- ◆ the year you were born
- ◆ your phone number
- ◆ your zip code
- ◆ your house or apartment number
- ◆ the grade you are in at school
- ◆ the number of people in your family
- ◆ your height in inches or centimeters

On another set of cards, write the Roman numerals for the same things.

Shuffle the cards well and arrange them face down. Then, take turns flipping over two cards at a time. If you make a match, you get to keep the cards. Otherwise, turn them face down again. The player who ends up with the most matches wins!

IN A WORD

You can use Roman numerals to spell three 3-letter words in English. Can you figure out what they are? (To get started, write down all the letters used for Roman numerals.) Which one of the three words translates into a real Roman numeral number? Compare your answers to the ones at the bottom of the page.

In a Word: DIM, LID, and MIX. MIX is the one that equals a real number: 1,009.

Send A Secret Code Message

Secret codes can come in handy, and they're lots of fun to use! Here's a quick code that uses numbers and your name.

1. Turn a piece of paper so that the long edge is at the top. Print the alphabet across the top.

2. The first letter of your name is number 1. For example, if your name is Melissa, write 1 under the letter M. Write 2 below the letter N, and so on until you reach Z, which will be 14 if your name begins with M. At that point, go to the letter A and write 15. Continue until you have given all 26 letters a number.

A	B	C	D	E	F	G	H	I	J	K	L	M	N	O
15	16	17	18	19	20	21	22	23	24	25	26	1	2	3

P	Q	R	S	T	U	V	W	X	Y	Z
4	5	6	7	8	9	10	11	12	13	14

☆ She said WHAT?

How about deciphering this message from Melissa? Check the bottom of the page for the answer.

1-15-6-25, 1-19-19-8 1-19 15-8 15-2-2'7.

Now, write a code using your name, putting 1 at the first letter of your name. Share your code with a friend and send secret messages back and forth.

PONDER SOME PATTERNS

Have you ever heard of math described as "the science of patterns"? Some folks believe that's exactly what math is. After you explore some patterns we use every day, and uncover the secrets behind them, you can decide if you agree.

Secret-Code Message: Mark, meet me at Ann's.

Faster Snail Mail

As businesses used the mail to send advertisements, catalogs, bills, and products to customers, the U.S. Postal Service needed a coding system to speed up the sorting process. On July 1, 1963, the ZIP (**Z**one **I**mprovement **P**lan) code gave every address in America a five-digit code. Take, for instance, the zip code for Charlotte, Vermont: 05445.

0 THE FIRST DIGIT REPRESENTS A BROAD U.S. REGION, WITH **0** FOR THE NORTHEAST AND **9** FOR THE WEST COAST

54 THE NEXT TWO DIGITS SPECIFY A LARGER POSTAL CENTER FOR THAT REGION

45 THE LAST TWO DIGITS PINPOINT SMALLER POST OFFICES THAT ARE PART OF A LARGER ZONE

054 Area

Charlotte, VT 05445

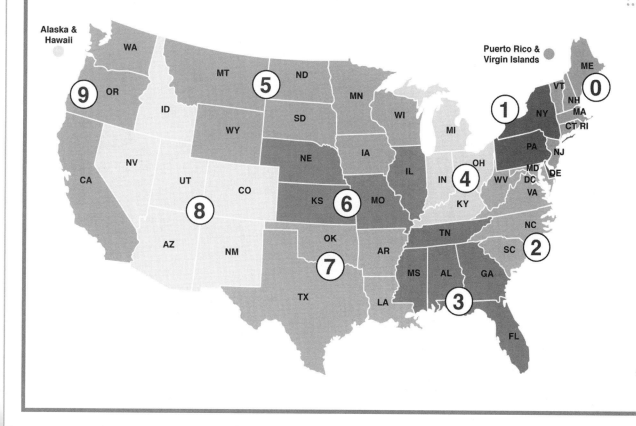

In 1983, four more digits were added to zip codes. Used mostly by businesses, they represent very specific locations, such as city blocks, post office boxes, or even office buildings. That's right — some big buildings have their own zip codes!

Fibonacci Numbers

One of the greatest mathematicians in history, Leonardo Fibonacci, was born in Pisa, Italy, more than 800 years ago. When he was a boy, his family lived in Algeria, Africa, where people used Arabic numbers (1, 2, 3, 4, 5 …). He was fascinated with these "new" numbers and made lots of discoveries about them. For example, he identified a special mathematical *sequence* (order) that starts with the following numbers: 1, 1, 2, 3, 5, 8, 13.

That's cool. When I add any two numbers that are next to each other, I get the next number. I wonder what that means...?

Math Marvel! ★

Fibonacci Fruits and Vegetables

So, who cares? What's so special about Fibonacci numbers? Well, they're significant because they reflect many patterns in nature.

The next time you have a banana, tomato, or cucumber, slice it horizontally and count the seed sections inside — it'll be a Fibonacci number!

To learn about the cool ways Fibonacci numbers turn up in nature, check out the website **<www.ee.surrey.ac.uk/personal/ r.knott/fibonacci/fibnat.html#seeds>**.

Moonbeam Coriopsis
8 petals

White Daisy
34 petals

Orange Zinnia
13 petals

Apple
5 seed segments

Orange
8 sac segments

☆ Be a Detective!

Unlock the mystery of Fibonacci numbers. Remember: There is only one set of Fibonacci numbers, and that set always begins at 1. (You cannot create a new series beginning with another number.)

*Examine the numbers in the Fibonacci series: **1, 1, 2, 3, 5, 8, 13.** Note that the second number is also "1." (If there were a number before the first 1, what might it be?) Can you guess what the next number in the series should be? Look at the relationships between the numbers. After you've had a turn at unlocking the mystery, compare your answer with the one at the bottom of this page.*

Be a Detective!: The next number is 21. To get each new number, you add the previous two together. If there were a number before 1, it would be 0. (0 + 1 = 1; 1 + 1 = 2; 2 + 1 = 3; 3 + 2 = 5; and so on.)

Stamp a Fibonacci T-Shirt

If you cut an apple in half sideways across the middle (not from the stem down), you'll find seeds in the shape of a five-pointed star. Five — that's a Fibonacci number! That star, which is really a cluster of seed casings around the apple's core, also makes a great stamp for a Fibonacci T-shirt.

WHAT YOU NEED

Scissors

Cardboard

Prewashed T-shirt

Paring knife

Apple

Paper towels

Nontoxic fabric paint, in separate containers

Paintbrush

Newspaper

WHAT YOU DO

1. Trim the cardboard so that it fits inside the shirt. (This will keep the paint from seeping through.)

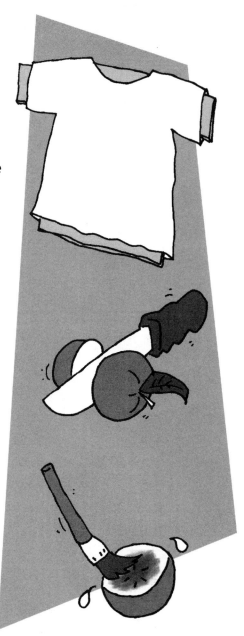

2. To prepare the apple for stamping, ask an adult to slice it in half horizontally; then blot the cut surfaces on paper towels.

3. Paint the cut surface of one of the fruit halves (you can eat the other half).

4. Practice your stamping technique on newspaper. Press down firmly and evenly; then lift the fruit stamp straight up. Once you've got the hang of it, you can stamp a Fibonacci number design on your shirt. If you want to switch colors, rinse off the paintbrush and the fruit (and blot it dry again) before painting on a new color.

5. For the finishing touch, use the tip of the paintbrush and a darker shade of paint to add five seeds — there's that Fibonnaci number again! — to your fruit prints.

6. Let the paint dry completely. Ask an adult to help you heat-set it with an iron according to the instructions for your fabric paint. Your Fibonnaci fruit fashion is now ready to wear!

1, 2, BUCKLE MY SHOE...

Real-World Patterns

Here are some number patterns that we use every day in the real world. Can you guess what they are?

A. 1, 1, 2, 3, 5, 8, 13, 21, 34, 55

B. 1, 2, 4, 8, 16, 32, 64

C. 1, 1, 1, 2, 1, 1, 1, 1, 1, 2, 1, 1, 1, 2, 1, 1, 1, 1, 1, 2

D. 31, 28, 31, 30, 31, 30, 31, 31, 30, 31, 30, 31

Real-World Patterns: A. Fibonacci numbers; B. cell division (doubling in number); C. pattern of black and white keys on a piano (starting with black, i.e. one black, one white, etc.); D. number of days in each of the twelve months.

Symmetry Surprises

★ Nature Knows!

Go on a symmetry search indoors and out. Look at the shapes of trees, shells, animals, and flowers for starters. How have humans given balance to their world by copying nature's symmetrical patterns?

Now that you've discovered patterns in Fibonacci numbers and piano keys, don't forget to look in the mirror. That's right, many living things — insects, animals, and even humans — have a natural kind of pattern or shape called *symmetry*. Look in the mirror and see for yourself. What features do each side of your body share?

If you look at a butterfly up close, you'll see that the pattern on both wings is exactly the same — as if one is a mirror reflection of the other. When a pattern or shape is reflected on either side of a line, it's called *bilateral symmetry* (*bi* meaning "two," and *lateral* meaning "sides").

Oops!

Tessellation Sensation

You can use symmetry to create a fascinating type of mathematical art that plays tricks on your eyes. It's called *tessellation*, and it's done by arranging squares in a checkered or mosaic pattern. When you look at it for a minute or two, you suddenly notice a pattern you didn't see before!

WHAT YOU NEED

Black construction paper

Ruler

Scissors

Cookie cutter

Colored poster board

Glue stick

WHAT YOU DO

1. Cut out ten 3" (7.5 cm) squares from the black construction paper.

2. Fold one of the squares in half diagonally; then spread it flat. Center the cookie cutter on the fold and trace around it.

3. Cut in from the corners along the fold to the top and bottom of the tracing, and then around one side of the tracing.

4. Use the larger of the cutout halves as a pattern for cutting the other nine squares. (You can stack a few and cut them together.)

5. Glue the cutouts onto the poster board, alternating the two different shapes to create four rows of five.

Play with Number Sequences

Create Your Own

Start with zero. Add 1. Add 2 to your answer. Then, add 3 to that number. Add 4, and so on to your answer, up until 9. The number sequence will add up to 165.

Start with zero. Add 10, subtract 5, add 10, subtract 5, and so on until your total is 150.

Start with zero. Add 2, multiply by 2, add 2, and multiply by 2. Continue until you reach 218.

Sequence Necklace

Turn a number sequence into beaded jewelry! That's right, *sequence* is just a fancy word for pattern, and patterns are all around us everyday!

WHAT YOU NEED

Paper and pencil

Calculator

Elastic beading thread

Tape

Pony beads, several different colors

WHAT YOU DO

1. Experiment with a few different number sequences by writing them down. The sequence should include 8 to 10 numbers that add up to between 125 and 175.

2. Decide how many different bead colors you want to use. To do this, divide the number of numbers in your sequence by a number that comes out evenly. (If there are 10 numbers in your sequence, as there are in the possible patterns provided to the left, you could use 2, 5, or 10 different colors.)

3. Attach a piece of tape to one end of your elastic thread to keep the beads from falling off.

Number sequences: First series: 0, 1, 3, 6, 10, 15, 21, 28, 36, 45; **second series:** 0, 10, 5, 15, 10, 20, 15, 25, 20, 30; **third series:** 0, 2, 4, 6, 12, 14, 28, 30, 60, 62.

4. Thread the beads, changing colors for each number in your sequence. If you were using the Fibonacci sequence, you would string on 1 white bead, 1 blue bead, 2 green beads, 3 red beads, 5 black beads, 8 white beads, 13 blue beads, 21 green beads, and 34 red beads, finishing with 55 black beads.

5. Remove the tape, tightly tie together the thread ends, and trim them. Now your necklace is ready to wear! Ask your friends if they can figure out the mathematical message in your necklace.

Anatoly Evgenievich Karpov learned the moves of chess when he was just 4 years old! Pretty impressive, since to win you need to come up with a sequence of moves that will trap your opponent's king.

At 15, Anatoly became the youngest player ever to win the Russian title of National Master!

If you're driving on a U.S. highway, you don't need a compass to tell you the direction you're heading in.

Interstates (marked by blue signs with red tops) and U.S. routes (posted on white signs with black numbers) that run east/west are *even-numbered*. *Odd-numbered* interstates and routes run north/south. What's more, interstate numbers get higher the farther east or north you travel, while U.S. route numbers get higher as you head west or south. (Hint: Remember that when you face north, west is on your left, east is on your right, and south is behind you. Also, when you look at a map, check out the key in the corner. Usually, the main roads are drawn in red and the secondary roads are in black.)

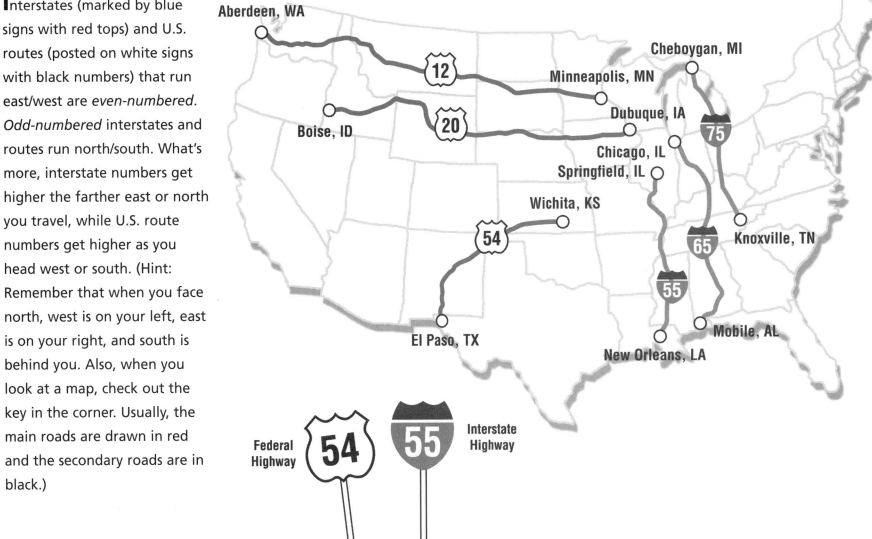

⭐ Are we heading north?

Here's a set of driving instructions from a town in one U.S. state to a location in a different state. Can you tell which direction these roads will take you? When you're done, compare your answer to the one at the bottom of the page.

- *Get on I-90 where it merges with U.S. Route 151. Follow the road to I-43.*
- *Take I-43 until it merges with I-141. Follow I-141 to U.S. Route 2.*
- *Follow U.S. Route 2 until you come to I-75.*
- *Take I-75 to U.S. Route 27.*
- *Take U.S. Route 27 to the state capital; then take I-69 to I-96.*
- *From I-96, take U.S. Route 131 into the city.*

Here's how it works in Canada:

- ◆ The provincial highways are numbered from 3 to 148.
- ◆ Secondary highways connecting towns and remote areas to larger highways are numbered from 503 to 673.
- ◆ The most rural roadways are numbered in the low 800s.

Provincial
(Saskatchewan)

Secondary
(Ontario)

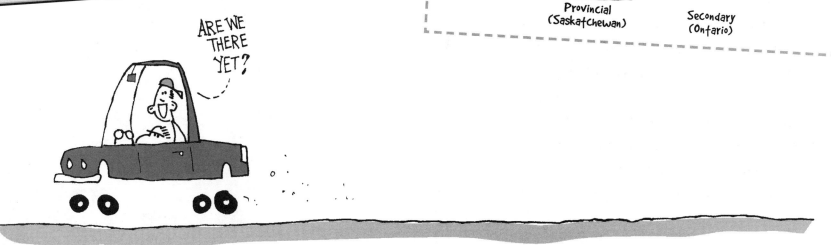

ARE WE THERE YET?

Numbering the Highways: You'd be traveling east on Routes 90 and 2, north on Routes 43 and 141, south on Routes 75, 27, 69, and 131, and west on Route 96 (from Madison, Wisconsin, to Grand Rapids, Michigan, by way of Michigan's Upper Peninsula.)

Route It Out

You probably know that the shortest distance between two places is a straight line. But when you're traveling, there are other factors to consider — such as speed limits, road conditions, and traffic — before choosing the route you want to take. Suppose, for example, that you're pulling out of your driveway in Sioux City, Iowa, to visit your grandparents in Minneapolis, Minnesota, when you hear on the radio that a huge winter storm is sweeping east across the Dakotas. Hmmm … that may affect your choice of routes!

You had planned to take Routes 60 and 169. That way, you would only have had to travel about 275 miles. Now you are considering heading east on U.S. Route 20 and then picking up Interstate 35 north, a route that is about 340 miles, which means an extra hour in the car.

Why would you ever consider the longer trip? If you were the driver, what would you do?

A Crossword Frenzy

Shortly after newspaper editor Arthur Wynne thought of using numbers to key the clues of a word puzzle he was preparing for the December 21, 1913, edition of the *New York World*, crossword puzzles became such a craze that libraries set a five-minute limit on using the dictionary!

Making up your own word puzzle can be just as much fun as solving one, particularly if you base your puzzle theme around one of your interests.

1. Pick a theme. For the example here, I chose football. On a sheet of graph paper (or make squares by drawing vertical and horizontal lines on a sheet of lined paper), print a word that relates to your theme (I started with *touchdowns*) so that one letter is in each box. (Hint: Start away from the margins so you'll have plenty of room to add words in all directions.)

2. Come up with another word that includes one of the letters from the first word. Write it down in such a way that the two words intersect at the shared letter.

3. Continue to add words until you've written at least five horizontally and five vertically. The trick is making sure that no letters other than the shared ones land in a box next to one that already contains a letter, because in a crossword, the words must *all* make sense, whether they're read across or down.

4. Cover your puzzle with tracing paper and outline all the boxes that have letters in them. This creates the empty grid for your puzzle.

5. Starting in the top left corner and working across one row at a time, number *only the boxes in which a word begins* (either across or down).

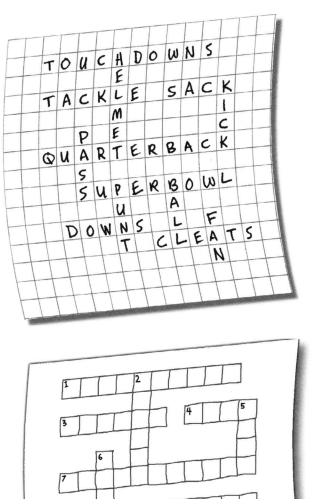

6. Write a list of clues for the words that go across and another list for the ones that go down. Now, see how long it takes someone to solve your puzzle!

ACROSS

1. How points are earned
3. How to stop the runner
4. Tackling the quarterback before he passes the ball or runs forward
7. The player who calls signals and directs offensive play
8. Winning this secures the world championship
11. There are four of these before a team loses the ball
13. Football footgear

DOWN

2. Protective headgear
5. Start the game by doing this to the ball
6. How you move the ball from player to player
9. One thing you can do on fourth down
10. Previously made of pigskin
12. Someone who loves the game intensely

Math Marvel! ★

★ ### A Word Record!

No one could ever describe Robert Turcot of Quebec, Canada, as clueless. In July 1982, he created a crossword puzzle that was bigger than 38 square feet (3.5 square meters). It contained 12,489 words across and 13,125 words down!

LEARN COMPUTER

English may be one of the six official languages of the United Nations, but computers still don't understand it! That's why people have developed special languages to communicate with computers. In "computerese," every letter, number, and punctuation mark is translated into an eight-digit sequence of zeros and ones. Each sequence is called a *byte*. For fun, see if you can translate this name — 01001011010000101010101100100100101001110 — back into English. (Hint: Begin by dividing the sequence after every eighth number.) The answer is at the bottom of the next page.

A	01000001		**N**	01001110
B	01000010		**O**	01001111
C	01000011		**P**	01010000
D	01000100		**Q**	01010001
E	01000101		**R**	01010010
F	01000110		**S**	01010011
G	01000111		**T**	01010100
H	01001000		**U**	01010101
I	01001001		**V**	01010110
J	01001010		**W**	01010111
K	01001011		**X**	01011000
L	01001100		**Y**	01011001
M	01001101		**Z**	01011010

LINGO

@ CHOO!

INTERNET VIRUS →

☆ **Do you write "computerese"?**

Now try writing your own name in computer language. Then, for a spooky message, decode the bytes written here, and compare your answer with the one below. (Hint: Count off every eight digits to see where each letter begins and ends.)

**01001000010000010101000001010000010
110010100100001000001010011000100011
000100111101010101110100010101000101 0
1001110**

Computerese: The spooky message is "Happy Halloween."

Computer Lingo: The name written in computer bytes is "Kevin."

Real-World Math™

Lots of Languages

About 5,000 languages are spoken in the world today! Chinese is the one used by the largest number of people — about one billion of them — while certain Australian Aboriginal dialects are spoken by as few as six people. But the one language everyone on planet Earth shares is the language of numbers, because no matter where you live and how you say it — *one, uno, un, yi, en* — 1 means the same thing the whole world over!

THE SHAPE OF THINGS

Just as numbers are the *words* that let us speak the language of math, shapes like squares, triangles, and circles are the *vehicles* — let's call them "spaceshapes" — that launch us into a whole new mathematical dimension.

We have learned a lot from observing these geometric shapes in the natural world. Picture a beehive's honeycomb. The six-sided wax cells fit together perfectly, preventing dirt and enemies from getting in, while providing maximum storage space for honey. Seeing how well these cells fit together has helped food distributors develop more efficient packaging for many of the foods we buy at the supermarket. You've seen the egg cartons and plastic trays with compartments for cookies? Those foods are packaged in similar "cells."

Mathematicians and scientists are continually using the things they learn about shapes in nature to come up with handy inventions. A bottle of roll-on antiperspirant works the same way as the ball-and-socket joints in our bodies do. And so does a ballpoint pen.

So, get ready to discover lots of things about geometric shapes. Test the strength of triangles to build roofs, create an arch for bridges the way ancient Romans did, and make symmetrical designs the same way Mother Nature does!

Reading Traffic Signs

In addition to directing the flow of cars and other vehicles, traffic signs tell drivers about road hazards and roadway services. Long before you can read them, you can often tell what signs are going to say just by looking at their shapes.

Squares and rectangles are for REGULATIONS, such as one way or do not pass.

A diamond shape signals a WARNING, such as a sharp curve or a deer crossing.

An upside-down triangle says YIELD (or give way) to oncoming traffic.

An octagon means STOP.

A circular sign represents a RAILROAD CROSSING.

Entering Another Dimension

Hold a penny on its edge and give it a quick twist to make it spin like a top on the floor. See how what resembled a flat circle an instant ago now looks like a round sphere — kind of like a miniature globe?

Here's what happens when you transform *two-dimensional* shapes (that appear flat) into *three-dimensional* objects.

□ = ▨

▭ = ▱

△ = ◭

○ = ● OR ⬭

SQUARING OFF

☆ Pack & stack shapes

Squares and rectangles are two of the best shapes for using space efficiently. Take a look around your home for squares and rectangles that you can play with (ask first!). Try stacking them in spacesaving ways in a paper shopping bag. Then, ask if you can experiment with cans from the kitchen cabinet. Try stacking the cans in the same paper bag. Which are easier to pack and stack?

What do a hopscotch grid, a downtown, and a pan of brownies have in common? They're usually divided into blocks — either squares or rectangles. With four corners and four sides that are all the same length, squares line up and stack neatly. Rectangles stack neatly, too; the only difference is that their sides are longer.

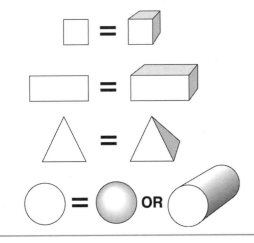

Balance a Glass on a Grain of Salt

When you draw four equal lines in the shape of a box, you've drawn a square. What if you wanted to turn that square into a three-dimensional shape? If you did, you'd end up with a cube that has six sides.

Did you know you stare at thousands of cubes every day in your kitchen without knowing it? Yep! They're in the salt shaker on the table! If you look at a grain of salt through a magnifying glass, you'll see that it's actually a perfectly shaped cube. Grains of salt may be tiny, but they're all you need to pull off this impressive feat.

1. Sprinkle some salt on a tabletop. (You don't need much!)

2. Carefully and slowly try to balance a drinking glass so that it comes to rest at an angle *against* one of the grains. It may not seem possible at first, but keep at it!

3. Step back and watch as unsuspecting passersby wonder why the glass doesn't topple over. Can you explain why?

How Many Squares in the Square?

The next time you're in the mood for saltines, try some fun with them first. Arrange 16 crackers in four rows of four to create a big square. Take a good look. How many squares do you see altogether — 17? 21? 22? Keep looking. When you think you've found them all, compare your answer with the one at the bottom of the page.

Sometimes when we look at something, we can see one big picture; other times we focus on the details. For example, if you were to magnify a picture on a computer screen, you would see thousands of tiny, colored squares called *pixels*. Since the pixels are way too small for us to see individually, the computer uses patterns of these pixels to create the big pictures you see on the screen. So what did you see in the square crackers — the big picture or the little details?

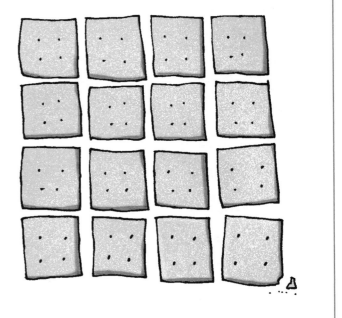

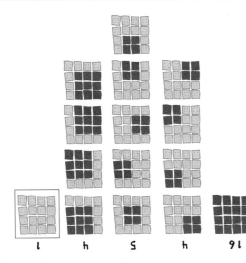

Squares in the Square: There's a total of 30! Can you come up with even more?
Hint: Look for squares *inside* each cracker. You'll find 81 more (nine per cracker).

1   4   5   4   16

Polly would really like a cracker... if you ever figure that out!

Send Postcard Puzzles

Send your friends fun greetings that will give them a real challenge. Find or make a picture postcard that you think a friend would like. Write a message on the back and then turn it into a puzzle by using this really neat math trick and a ruler.

WHAT YOU NEED

Picture postcard (4" x 6"/10 x 15 cm)

Ruler

Pencil or marker

Scissors

WHAT YOU DO

1. Place the postcard (picture side down) on a table so that the long sides are on the top and bottom. Lay a ruler down perpendicular so that the measurement marks for whole inches (cm) line up with the top and bottom edges of the postcard. Mark all the inch (cm) spots between the edges.

2. Now slide the ruler toward the opposite end of the postcard. Line up the measurement marks again and mark where the inches (cm) fall. Then draw straight horizontal lines, using the two marks for each line as a guide.

3. Turn the postcard on end and repeat the last two steps so you can draw vertical lines.

4. Cut along all the lines — and presto! You have a picture puzzle of equal-sized pieces. Put them in an envelope and mail your surprise!

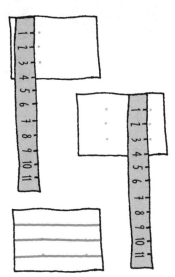

TREMENDOUS TRIANGLES

Sometimes more is less. Take a triangle, for instance. It has only three sides, but it's stronger than a square. Can you believe it? That's because a triangle's sides push against each other with equal force to keep the shape from collapsing under pressure. A pitched roof has wooden triangles under its shingles — that's why it doesn't cave in under heavy rain or snow.

Real-World Math

Terrific Tetrahedrons

Your basic tetrahedron

What happens when you turn a triangle into a three-dimensional shape? You create a *tetrahedron* (teh-tra-HEE-drun). It has four faces, each of which is a triangle. Use toothpicks and gumdrops or mini-marshmallows to build a tetrahedron to test the strength of triangular construction.

1. Firmly push the tips of three toothpicks into three gumdrops or mini-marshmallows to create a basic triangle.

2. With two more toothpicks and one gumdrop or mini-marshmallow, attach an adjoining triangle.

3. Add one more toothpick to finish the tetrahedron.

4. Add more and more triangles to build a bridge or a tower. Then, test its strength by seeing if it can hold up a book or two.

Towering Triangles

When Alexander Gustave Eiffel designed and built the famous Eiffel Tower in Paris, he used a series of open triangles called *trusses*. Because triangles can withstand a lot more pressure than other shapes, he believed that they could support the tremendous weight of the tower. And he figured that the gusty winds could blow right through the triangles instead of blowing the tower down. He was right! The tower never sways more than 5" (12.5 cm), even in a howling wind, despite the fact that it's about as high as a 100-story skyscraper! (How many floors does your house or apartment building have? Now imagine how high it would be if it were 100 stories high!)

Eiffel Tower ▪ Paris, France

TESTING TRIANGLES FOR
S T R E N G T H

Using wood glue, connect three Popsicle sticks together into a triangle. Then, add two sticks to one side of it to make another triangle (this one will be upside down). Make another one next to that triangle for three triangles in a row. Keep adding sticks to make more triangles. After the glue dries, wiggle it. Is it rigid?

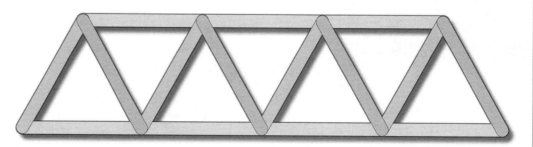

Hey, you've made what bridge builders call a *truss,* a framework made by joining straight pieces into triangles. Trusses are used in bridges to add strength and stability. Compare the strength of your truss by using more Popsicle sticks to make three squares in a row. Wiggle it after it dries. Which series of shapes do you think is stronger — the triangles or the squares?

YAY!

YAY!

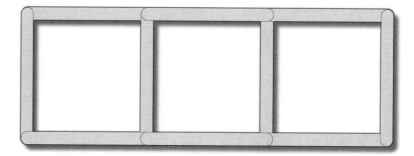

AMAZING ARCHES

You see them everywhere! Many windows — old and new — are shaped like arches; some walkways are trellised with arches covered in flowers; many gates and entrances are shaped like arches. Why? Because arches are considered by many to be one of the most beautiful shapes in construction, and they are certainly one of the strongest.

St. Louis Arch ▪ St. Louis, Missouri

It's on backorder.

BUILD AN ARCH, ROMAN-STYLE!

The Romans, who ruled over much of Europe for 500 years between the first century B.C. to the fourth century A.D. (see page 82), were the first great arch bridge builders. They added stones to both sides, higher and higher along the curve until only one stone, called the *keystone*, was needed at the top.

The Romans realized long ago that it's impossible to make an arch without supporting it as it goes up. They used a wooden frame, called the *centering*, to support arches as they were being built. The centering was removed after the keystone was in place.

★ Build your own amazing arch!

To build a Roman-style arch, you'll need some clay or Play-Doh and a bunch of small rocks. Use something as the centering for your stone and clay bridge, such as a block that's the right shape. Or try cutting up a cylindrical container (a long circle like a tube), such as a round oatmeal container, to get a curved surface. Then, using the clay as cement, fit the rocks together over the centering to form your arch.

Rainbow Bridge ▪ *Rainbow Bridge Park, Utah*

Let a Rainbow Be Your Teacher

Remember those honeycombs that helped food distributors repackage their products? How do you think ancient peoples may have gotten the idea for curved arches? Perhaps from seeing the shape in nature — a rainbow, the entrance to a cave, or a natural rock formation like the Rainbow Bridge in southeastern Utah. It took millions of years for moving water to carve this arch out of pink sandstone. The Navajo people called it *Nonnezoshe* (non–NAY–zho–eh–zhay), which means "the rainbow turned to stone."

Look closely at Rainbow Bridge, noticing how its ends are thicker than the top, like a man-made arch. (Or is it that the man-made arch is just like nature's?)

SPLENDID CIRCLES

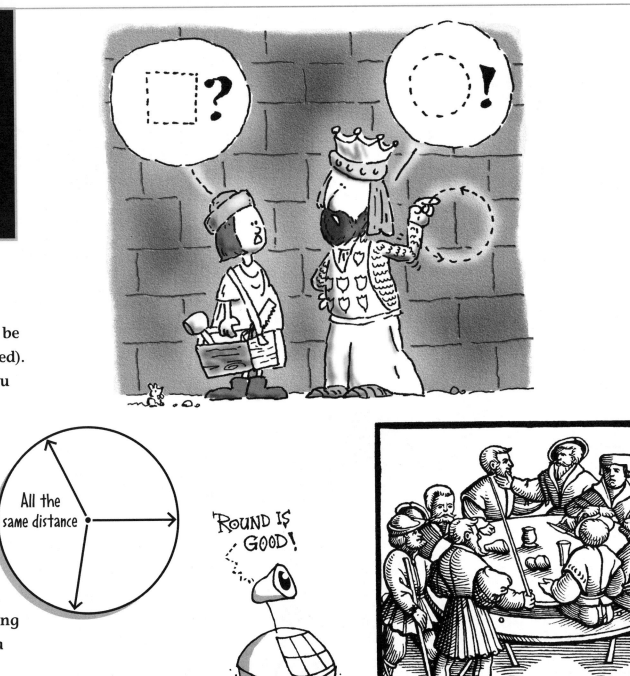

If you were to name a shape that's handiest all around, it would have to be the circle (no pun intended). How smooth a ride do you think you'd have if your bike or school bus had square tires? Circles and spheres are different from any other geometric shape because every point along the outside is an equal distance from the center. That's the very reason King Arthur's knights met at a round table — all of the seats were considered equally important.

All the same distance

'ROUND IS GOOD!'

CIRCLE LINGO

To get around circles, you may need to add a few special words to your vocabulary. Here are some that will help!

The **circumference** of a circle is the total distance around the outside of the circle.

The **diameter** of a circle is the total distance across the center of the circle from one side to the other.

The **radius** of a circle is the length from the center of a circle to the outside of a circle (this is always one-half of the diameter).

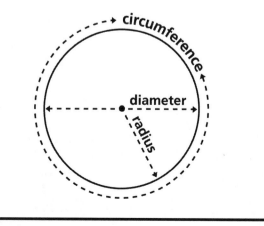

Step through a Sheet of Paper

"No way!" you say. A sheet of paper isn't even as big as your shirt, so even if you cut a huge hole in the middle, how could you possibly get your whole body through it? Perform a little math magic to turn a rectangle into a circle. All you need is a full sheet of construction paper, a ruler, and scissors.

1. Fold the paper in half lengthwise so that the long edges match up. Then, fold the paper in half crosswise four times in a row and flatten the creases with a ruler.

2. Unfold the paper, except for the first fold.

3. Starting at one end, cut along the first crease from the long center fold, stopping ½" (1 cm) from the other side. Snip the second crease from the opposite direction, stopping ½" (1 cm) from the center fold.

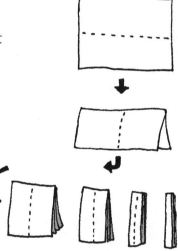

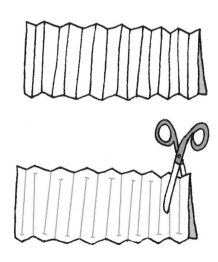

4. Continue cutting along the creases, alternating directions and stopping ½" (1 cm) from the side you're cutting toward.

5. Cut along the center fold of all the strips except the ones at each end.

6. Carefully pull apart the strips, and you'll have a circle large enough to step right through!

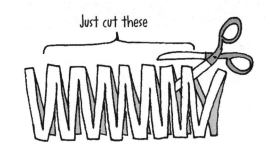

Just cut these

THE PERFECT CIRCLE

When Pope Bonaface VIII wanted to decorate the first St. Peter's Cathedral in Rome, Italy, in the early 1300s, he asked the great artists of the time for samples of their work. Giottodi Bondone convinced the pope that he was the best artist for the job. How did he do it? By using only one stroke to paint what appeared to be a perfect circle (a circle whose points on the circumference — or outside — are exactly the same distance from its center)!

It's beautiful!

⭐ Draw a "perfect" circle!

You, too, can draw what appears to be a perfect circle. All you need is a garden shovel, two sturdy sticks, and a rope that is about 8' (240 cm) long. Dig a hole in the dirt and firmly stake one of the sticks in the ground. Tie a loop in one end of the rope and slip it over the stake. (It should fit loosely.) Tightly tie the other end around the lower end of the second stick. Holding the second stick, walk away from the stake just until the rope is taut (not sagging). Then, keeping the rope taut, walk around the stake, drawing a line in the dirt with the stick. You'll end up with a circle that has a radius that's equal to the length of your rope.

P.S. How would you do the same thing on a piece of paper?

PIE TAG

Here's a fun game you and a few friends can play, using the circle-drawing method above. Remove the center stake and then draw lines across the circle and through the center to divide it into eight pie slices. Choose someone to be "it." Have her start in the center of the circle, while the other players stand anywhere on the edge of the circle. During the game, players can run in any direction as long as they stay on a pie line or on the circumference. The first person tagged becomes the next "it."

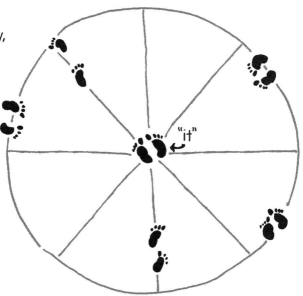

Want to make it really exciting? Play the exact same game in the snow and see how slippery your pie edges become!

Paint with a Pendulum

Imagine holding a small circle between your index finger and thumb and giving it a little squeeze. That's what an ellipse looks like — a slightly squashed circle. With a homemade pendulum, you can paint a cool pattern of ellipses. One warning: This activity is a blast, but it can get messy! Set it up outdoors and don't forget to put on an apron or an old shirt! Better yet, do it in the summer in your swimsuit and then hose down afterward.

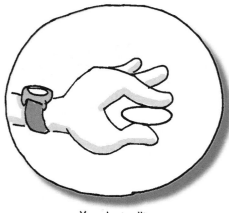

Your basic ellipse

WHAT YOU NEED

Plastic bottle with squirt cap (any size)

Scissors

Ball of sturdy string

Newspaper

White butcher paper (nonglossy)

Large measuring cup

Tempera paint

Water

Stick for mixing

WHAT YOU DO

1. Ask an adult to help you cut the bottom off the plastic bottle. Above the cut edge, make four equally spaced holes around the bottle through the plastic.

2. Cut four pieces of string about 2' (60 cm) long; thread one through each hole. Knot the ends to keep them from pulling back through the bottle.

3. Gather the tops of the strings and tie them to a clothesline, tree branch, or similar structure, so that your pendulum hangs about 3' (90 cm) above the ground.

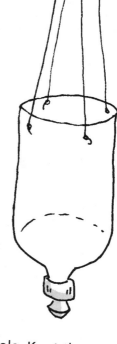

4. Make sure the bottle cap is screwed on tightly and the squirt top is closed.

5. Spread newspaper and then your paper on the ground underneath the pendulum.

6. Pour equal amounts of paint and water into a measuring cup and stir. Pour the mixture into the pendulum so that it's about two-thirds full.

7. Slowly pull the pendulum out to one side. Carefully and quickly open the nozzle and release the bottle. Step back and watch. The pendulum painter will draw a series of elliptical curves as it swings back and forth!

MORE ART FUN!

Change the paint colors and repeat the process. Change the size of the ellipse by making the strings on the bottle longer or shorter.

Traveling in Space

Earth, and all the other planets in our solar system, travel around the sun in elliptical orbits.

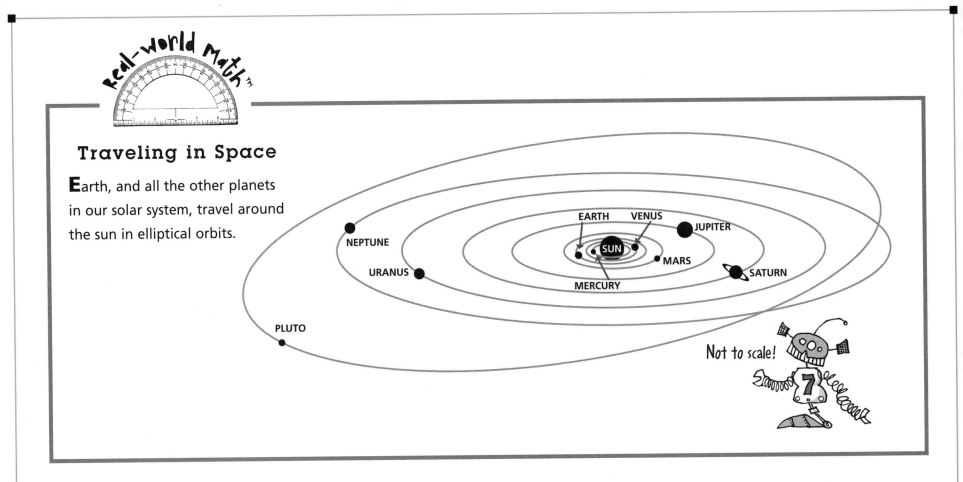

Not to scale!

Math Marvel ★

★

Popcoin!

A quarter would never fit through a dime-sized hole, right? Trace around a dime on a sheet of paper and cut out the inside of the circle. Now try to slip the quarter through the hole without tearing the paper. If you get frustrated, check out the solution on the next page. Then, challenge some friends to do the trick. Once they give up, amaze them by showing how it's done!

No way!

ROUND UP SOME CYLINDERS

If you take a two-dimensional circle and extend it into a column, you end up with a *cylinder*. *Silos*, the tall, round buildings in which farmers store cattle feed, are hollow cylinders. The cylindrical shape is a stronger structure than a tall, rectangular shape. Fresh grain goes in at the top and sinks to the bottom slowly and *evenly* because there are no corners or crossbeams in which the feed can build up. And can you name a toy that's shaped like a cylinder but can "walk" down stairs?

When Joe Bowen was a kid growing up in Bowen, Kentucky, he made great strides in math by turning a couple of cylinders (ordinary tin cans) into a pair of stilts. He became so good at stiltwalking that in 1980 he raised $100,000 for the Muscular Dystrophy Association by stiltwalking 3,008 miles home to Bowen from Los Angeles, California!

Popcoin!: Fold the paper in half across the diameter of the circle and sandwich the quarter between the halves. Slowly and gently pull the sides of the paper upward. The quarter will pop right through! That's because you've turned the circle into an ellipse, which has made the diameter of the hole bigger.

Dude!

Round Up Some Cylinders: A Slinky!

A Tiny Tumbler

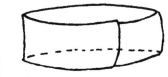

Here's how you can team up two different mathematical shapes in the circle family — a cylinder and a sphere — to put on a show that your friends will flip over.

WHAT YOU NEED

Heavy-weight paper

Ruler

Pencil

Scissors

Tape

Marble

Colored markers

WHAT YOU DO

1. Cut out a strip of paper that measures 1" x 5" (2.5 x 12.5 cm). Use it to form a cylinder, over-lapping one edge ¼" (5 mm) and taping it in place.

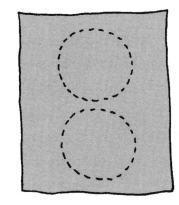

2. Set the short cylinder on top of the remaining paper and trace around it. Cut out the traced shape and use it as a pattern to cut out another one.

3. Tape one of the cutouts to the bottom of the cylinder. Insert a marble and tape the second cutout to the top.

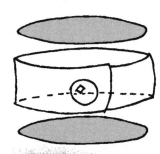

4. Set the piece upright so that it stands like a wheel. Draw a face on the front, and it's ready to roll. Set it on a slightly inclined surface and watch it go!

Your basic golden spiral...

SCOPING OUT SPIRALS

Your basic circle

Your basic spiral

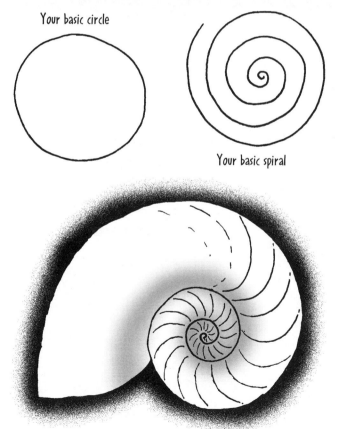

Ah, the spiral — one of nature's wonders! Unlike a circle, in which the line begins and ends in the same spot, a *spiral* is one long line in the form of a circle, in which the line gets farther and farther away from its starting point. Take a careful look around outside or in your house to find spirals in some clever hiding places — such as the spring in your flashlight!

There are some pretty amazing spirals in our world, from the tiny snail to those cyclones you watch on the news. How about the Milky Way? Did you know that's a spiral? So is a spider web. To make one, the spider starts in the center, then spins out a spiral, keeping an equal distance between each new turn. This is known as an *archimedean* (ark-I-MEED-ian) spiral. It connects the turns of the spiral with spokes, and the web becomes a perfect trap to catch the insects it will eat.

In an *equiangular* (ee-qui-ANG-ular) spiral, the distance between the coils gets wider and wider the farther out you go. A snail shell is constructed this way. As the snail grows, it adds onto its shell "house" in such a way that the outer edge enlarges faster than the inner edge to create a wider space for the animal's bigger body. How cool is that?

Make a Spinning Spiral

Here's a spinning spiral that will dance in your room when you turn on a lamp.

WHAT YOU NEED

Poster board

Pencil

Scissors

Colored markers

String

WHAT YOU DO

1. Draw a large circle on the poster board and cut it out.

2. Draw a spiral on the poster board and a cut line at the outer edge. Starting at the outer edge, cut along the line. Color a design on the spiral.

3. Make a small hole in the center of the spiral. Thread the string through it and knot the end to keep it from pulling through.

4. Ask an adult to help hang your spiral 12" (30 cm) or so above a lamp. Turn on the lamp. Warm air rising from the lightbulb will make it spin!

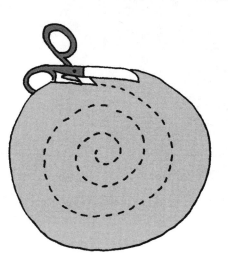

Real-World Math

PYRAMID POWER

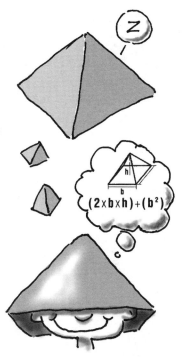

$$(2 \times b \times h) + (b^2)$$

▲ If you sleep inside a pyramid, you will not grow old.

▲ You can polish tarnished coins without rubbing them if you put them in a pyramid.

▲ Spend time in a pyramid, and you'll be able to see the future.

▲ Keep fruit and milk fresh by storing them in pyramids.

▲ To become smarter, cover your head with a pyramid.

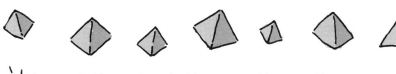

Ideas about the magical powers of pyramids have been around for thousands of years. Supposedly, a California dentist hangs a pyramid from the ceiling over his patients' heads. He believes that his patients get fewer cavities and heal faster because of it!

Once a young man decided to camp inside an ancient pyramid. He thought it might make him smarter. That night, he felt as if he couldn't breathe. Then, colored lights appeared before his eyes, and a "strange energy" seemed to enter his body. When he left, he felt very peaceful and said he felt he knew all there was to know.

Hmmm ... What do you think about his experience with pyramid power?

☆ Rectangle Power?

To see if pyramid power may be part of the real world, place one slice of raw fruit under a pyramid that you made and another equal-sized slice under a rectangle or square (like a shoe box). Which keeps the fruit fresh longer?

Create Clay Pyramids

To make a simple pyramid, press out some clay or Play-Doh into four triangles and one square. Make the base of the triangles the same length as the sides of the square. Make the other sides of the triangles all the same length. Then, place the base of each triangle onto the square and join them at the top. Press the seams of the walls together gently. You can make pyramids of different sizes as long as you carefully measure the sides of your triangles and squares so they match up correctly.

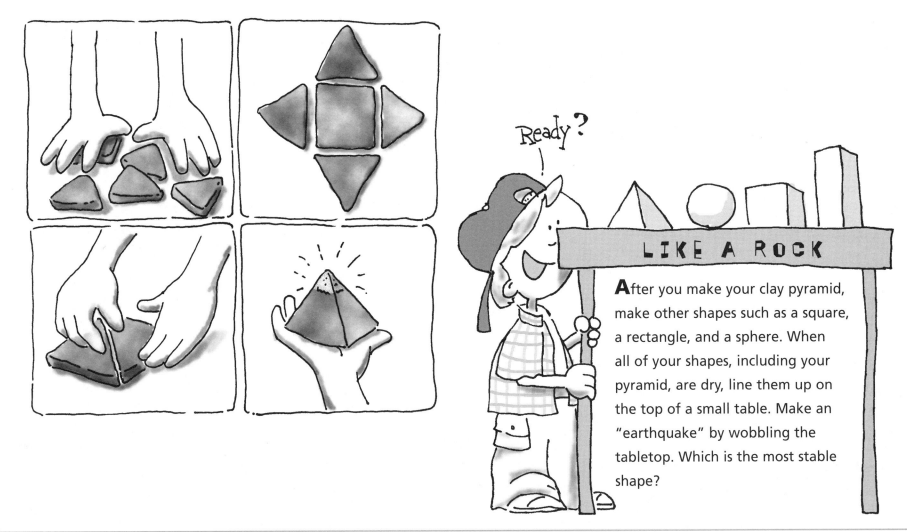

Ready?

LIKE A ROCK

After you make your clay pyramid, make other shapes such as a square, a rectangle, and a sphere. When all of your shapes, including your pyramid, are dry, line them up on the top of a small table. Make an "earthquake" by wobbling the tabletop. Which is the most stable shape?

Although pyramids can be found in many cultures around the world, Egypt's Great Pyramid of Giza — one of four that still remain there — is the grandest pyramid of all! It's so large that it can be seen from the moon! It's also the oldest structure still standing on the face of the earth, built about 4,600 years ago. When it was first built, the stones fit together so perfectly that even a piece of paper couldn't fit between them! Wow! Can you imagine how hard building that must have been without modern equipment?

You can build a miniature Egyptian-style temple of your own out of sugar cubes — no huffing and puffing required, just some basic multiplication to make sure you have the supplies you need.

WHAT YOU NEED

1½ cups (375 ml) confectioners' sugar

Mixing bowl

Measuring spoons

Spoon for mixing

Water

Sugar cubes

Cardboard or poster board

Butter knife or small plastic spatula

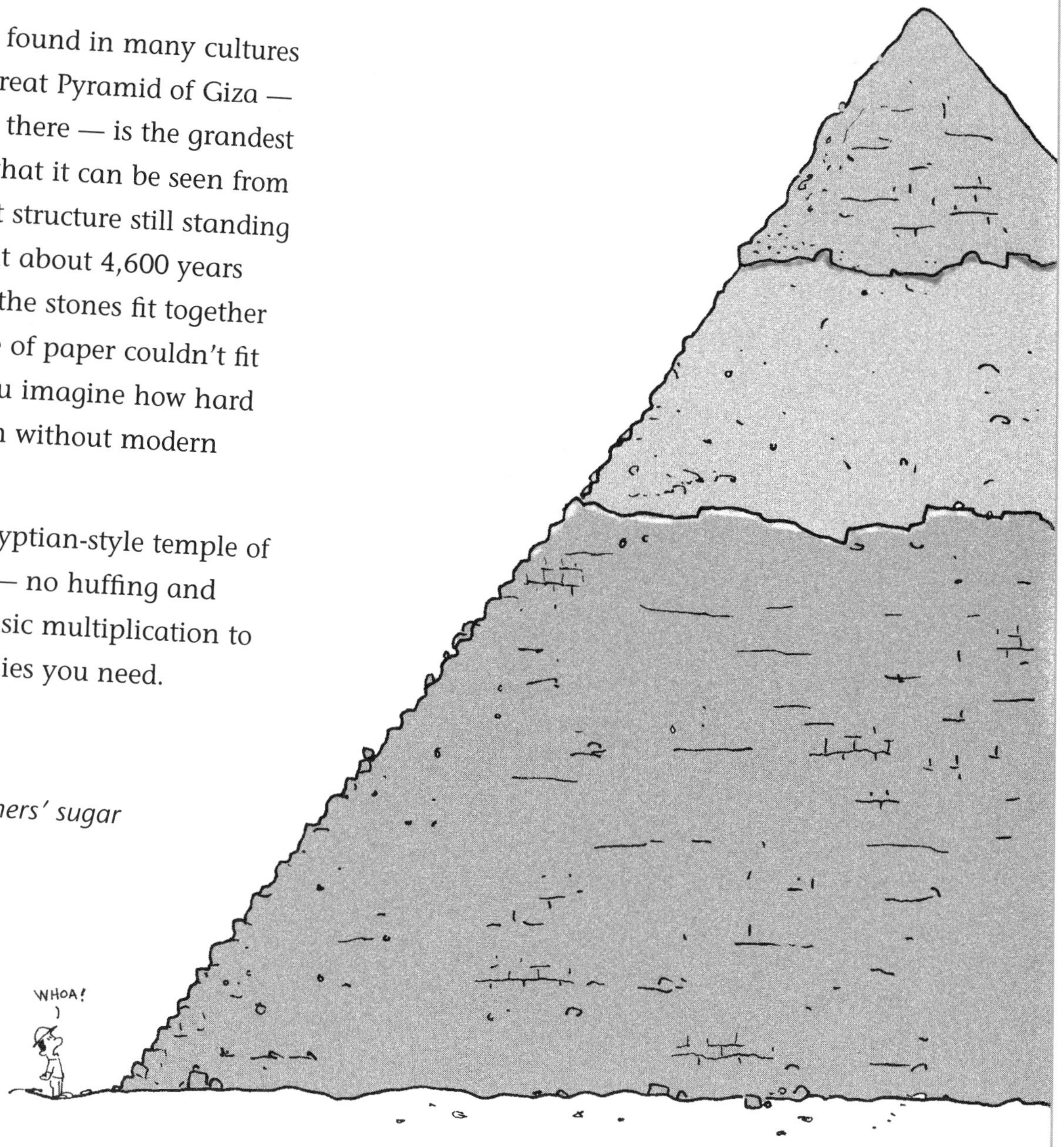

WHOA!

Great Pyramid ■ Giza, Egypt

WHAT YOU DO

1. Mix a batch of "mortar" by pouring the confectioners' sugar into a mixing bowl and adding just enough water to make the mixture moist but stiff. Start with four or five tablespoons (60 to 75 ml); add more as needed.

2. Once your "mortar" is the right consistency, spread it with a dull knife to cement together nine rows of nine sugar cubes that form a square base layer on the cardboard.

3. Cement a second layer of eight rows of eight cubes centered on top of the base.

4. On top of the second layer, add a layer that is seven cubes by seven cubes; then a layer that is six by six, five by five, and so on, until you can top off your pyramid with a single cube.

How Many Boxes of Sugar Cubes Do You Need?

1. Calculate the number of cubes you'll need for a base layer that's nine cubes by nine cubes. You'll actually be figuring out the *area* of the layer, which is the *length* times the *width* (L x W) — in this case, 9 x 9. (Try it first with four cubes. Lay four across and four down. Now fill in the layer. Did you use 16 cubes? There you go! 4 x 4 = 16; in other words, L x W = Area.)

2. You can do the same thing to come up with the number of cubes you'll need for the areas of the eight remaining layers. Just decrease the sides of the square by one cube with each layer.

3. Add all of the numbers you came up with. Divide the total by the number of cubes that come in a box (typically 198 in a one-pound box). How many boxes do you think you'll need?

Number of Sugar Cubes Needed

9 x 9 =	81	(base layer)
8 x 8 =	64	
7 x 7 =	49	
6 x 6 =	36	
5 x 5 =	25	
4 x 4 =	16	
3 x 3 =	9	
2 x 2 =	4	
1 x 1 =	+ 1	
	285	

3) 285 ÷ 198 = 1.4, or a little less than one and a half boxes, which means you'll have to buy two boxes.

Pyramid H U N T !

Pyramid shapes and pictures of pyramids are all around us. You can find pyramids on business signs and travel brochures, on TV, and in books and magazines. Do you think you can find pyramids three times in one day? You just might if you go on a pyramid hunt! (Hint: Start by looking at a U.S. $1 bill.)

Can I have a dollar? I'm looking for pyramids.

MEASURING UP

Imagine how hard it would be to buy new shoes if the sizes weren't printed in them; you'd be lacing and unlacing, lacing and unlacing, until at last, you happened to try on a pair that fit. Sounds frustrating, you say? Hmmm ... now that you mention it, think of how much time a certain prince might have saved searching for Cinderella if he could have narrowed down the glass slipper fittings to maidens with a specific shoe size. There you go — math can make things a lot easier to size up!

That's what this chapter is all about — seeing how things measure up. You can find out how much space a dinosaur would take up in your home and use measurements to make a birdhouse. There are a few surprises, too. (For instance, you'll find out how a grasshopper can jump farther than the star broad jumper on your school's track team!)

I was really looking for Something in a running shoe.

Make that a Quarter-Pounder — er — a 125-Grammer!

In September 1999, NASA's Mars Climate Orbiter orbited off course — just as it was (mistakenly) programmed to do! Some scientists believe it happened because one team of flight controllers had programmed the spacecraft using English units (used in the United States), while another team had used metric measurements (used in Canada)!

So why hasn't the United States adopted the metric system — conveniently based on multiples of 10 — the way the rest of the world has (especially since the U.S. National Bureau of Standards officially endorsed metrification way back in 1964)?

Some say the English units still used in the United States are easier. (Take, for example, that gallon of milk in your fridge; in metric terms, when it's gone, your mother might have to ask you to pick up 3.785 liters of milk at the store!) Some also say that it makes more sense; the foot was originally based on the length of a human foot, and a cup is roughly the amount you could hold in your cupped hands. Others claim it's more precise because it takes a greater number of smaller units to make up each larger unit. Consider the temperature span between freezing and boiling: You get a choice between 180° Fahrenheit (the English unit) but only 100° Celsius (the metric unit).

Yet, American technologists, goldsmiths, doctors, and pharmacists in the U.S. routinely work in metric measures that range from centi-meters to carats. What you do think? Should we keep inching along, so to speak, with English measurements, or is it time to take some substantial strides toward metrification?

Size Up Your Shoe Size

HOW BiG?

You may think that since you wear the same-size shoe on each of your feet that both of your feet are the same size. But that's not necessarily so.

1. Place a sheet of paper on the floor and step on it with one bare foot.

2. Make a pencil mark just above your big toe and another right behind your heel.

3. Measure between the two marks in inches or centimeters.

4. Now measure your other foot. Compare the results. Ask your family members or friends if you can conduct the experiment on them. What do you come up with?

5. Is there any relationship between the number of inches or centimeters your foot measures and the number shoe size you wear?

Math Marvel! ★

What's Bigger — Your Foot or Your Forearm?

You already know how long each foot is. Now take a quick look at your forearm (the length from your wrist to your elbow). Which do you think is longer? Measure them and see for yourself. Then, check your results with the answer at the bottom of the page.

Math Marvel: Believe it or not, they're usually the same length!

How Big Is Your Yard, Anyway?

Before your home was built, someone hired a surveyor to measure and mark the lot of land on which the house would be situated. Building lots are generally measured in acreage, and many cities and towns require that the lots be no smaller than a certain size in order to build. An acre of land can take many shapes — a square, a rectangle, or even a pie-slice wedge — but it must total 43,560 square feet (4,051 square meters).

What's the difference between a foot and a square foot? A foot is a measurement of *length* — a straight line that is 12" (30 cm) long. A square foot is the *area* that fits into a block that is 12" (30 cm) long and 12" (30 cm) wide. That area, however, can take many shapes. All that matters is that it equals the same area that fits a 12" x 12" (30 x 30 cm) square.

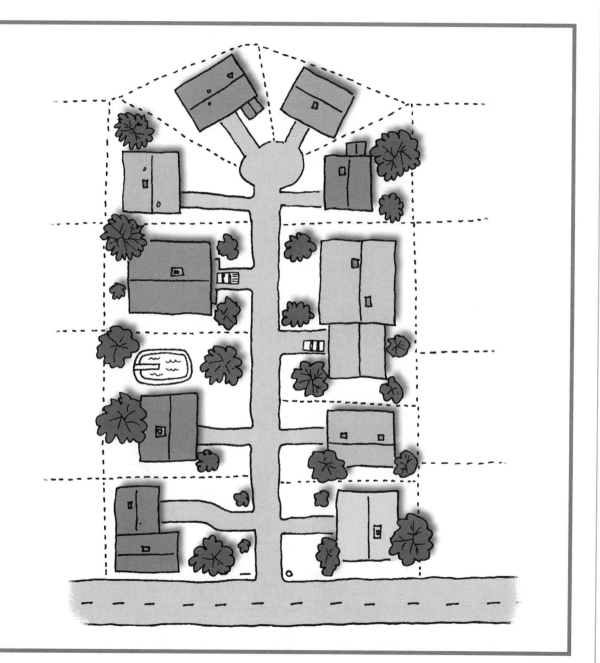

Could a Dinosaur Fit in Your Backyard?

That would depend on what kind of dinosaur you had in mind. A *Compsognathus* (comp-so-NA-thus), a birdlike meat eater, could probably fit on your bookshelf. It measured just 2' (60 cm) from its pointy head to the tip of its tail and weighed about 6½ pounds (2.5 kg). If you're talking about a *Brachiosaurus* (BRAW-kee-o-sore-us), well, that's a different story. It could grow up to 69' (21.25 m) long and 36' (11 m) tall. Here's a fun way to visualize just how huge that is.

WHAT YOU NEED

Ball of string or twine 100' (35 m) long

Yardstick (meterstick)

A friend

WHAT YOU DO

1. Head outdoors with a friend to measure the length of your house or apartment building from one side to the other. Starting at one corner, lay the yardstick (meterstick) down in front of the house. Measure (your friend can help) from one side to the other (and beyond) until you measure 69' (21.25 m). This is the length of a *Brachiosaurus*! How far past the corner of the house are you? How many of your houses built side by side would it take to equal the length of a *Brachiosaurus*?

Real-World Math

2. Now that you know how much space you'd need to reserve for a visiting *Brachiosaurus*, figure out how far above the roofline it would tower. Have an adult help you measure the height of a room on the first floor by measuring up one wall from the floor to the ceiling.

3. Divide this number into 36' (11 meters) — the height of your average visiting *Brachiosaurus*. That will tell you how many stories high your house would have to be to fit one of these visitors under your roof.

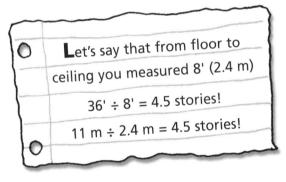

Let's say that from floor to ceiling you measured 8' (2.4 m)

36' ÷ 8' = 4.5 stories!

11 m ÷ 2.4 m = 4.5 stories!

Wow! That's one huge houseguest!

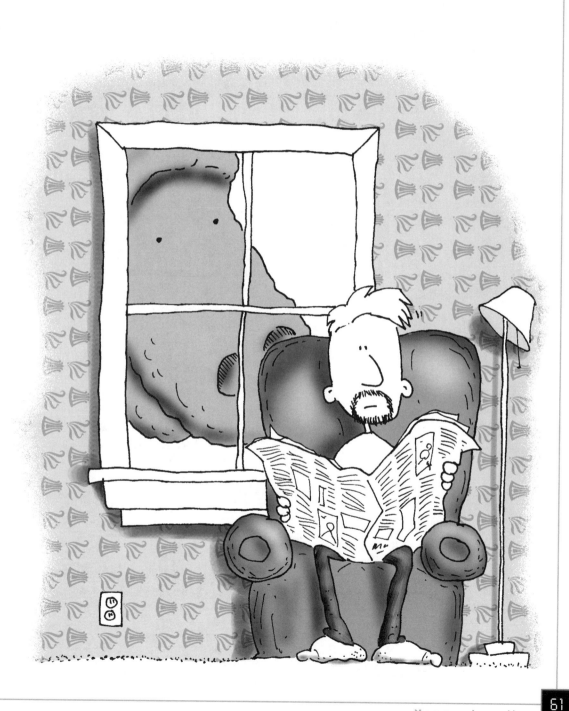

MAKING HOTEL Reservations

So, how long are you in town for?

"Ah, hello? May I reserve a football field for the weekend? The Seismosauruses are visiting!"

Yes, the *Seismosaurus* is even bigger than a *Brachiosaurus*!

As a school kid, George Washington didn't have an easy time with most subjects, but he measured up in math. By the time he turned 16 (in 1748), he was so good with numbers and shapes that he was hired to survey the wild territories of Virginia! (He put his surveying skills to use again 43 years later when, as our nation's first president, he measured out the boundaries for America's capital city.)

Hmmm...If cherry trees are $1.50 each...

My! You're Growing Like a Weed!

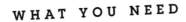

HOW HIGH?

Has an adult ever told you that you're growing like a weed? Of course, that doesn't mean you're sprouting green leaves. It's just a fun way to say that you seem to be growing as quickly as a plant. Some sunflowers, like the Gigantus or the Sungold, can grow up to 10' (3 m)! Here's an interesting way to chart the growth of sunflowers, pole beans, sweet potatoes, snap peas, cosmos flowers, or other fast-growing plants.

WHAT YOU NEED

Graph paper

Pencil

Metal tape measure

Seeds (giant sunflowers, pole beans, snap peas, cosmos flowers, trailing vines)

Planters or garden spot

WHAT YOU DO

1. Starting in the lower left corner of a sheet of graph paper and working up, chart the height of the plant from 0' to 2' (0 cm to 60 cm) so that each square equals 2" (5 cm).

2. Chart the time along the bottom of the page so that every seven squares equals one week.

3. Plant some seeds in a section of garden or a terra-cotta pot that you can place in a window that gets a lot of sun. Keep the seeds moist, but not wet, and wait for them to grow.

4. As soon as the seeds sprout, choose a couple of seedlings to chart. Leave one in the sun and transplant the other into a part of the yard that's shaded or into another terra-cotta pot placed in the shade. Water them both as needed and carefully measure the height of both plants in inches or centimeters. Plot the measurements with different colored markers at the end of Week 1 on the graph. Also note the weather that week. Was it sunny or overcast? Hot or cool? Dry or wet?

5. At the end of the next week, take new measurements and plot them on the graph, and draw a picture of the weather that week. As you add each week's measurements, connect the dots with lines in the appropriate colors.

6. When you've completed your graph, check it out. When did the plants grow fastest? What effect, if any, do you think the weather had? What differences do you notice between the plant that was in the sun and the one that was in the shade?

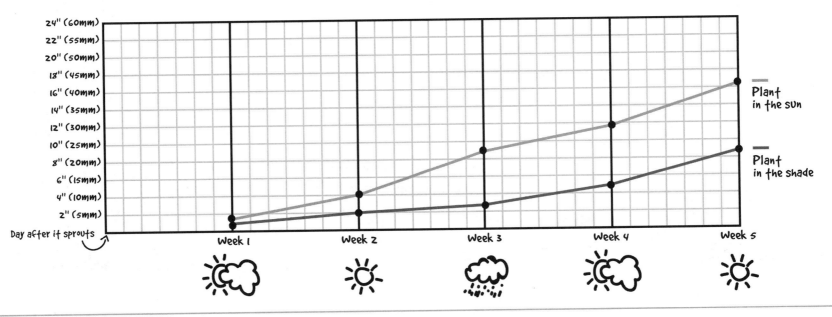

How High Is It?

Have you ever wondered how high trees are? Here's an easy way for you and a friend to figure it out without climbing to the top of one with a tape measure.

1. Ask your friend how tall she is. Then, have her stand right beside the trunk of the tree you want to measure.

2. Walk far enough away so that a yardstick (or meterstick) held at arm's length appears taller than the tree. Close one eye and line up the zero inch (0 cm) mark with your friend's feet. Read the measurement that lines up with the top of her head to see how many inches (cm) tall she is on the yardstick.

3. Keeping your arm steady and one eye closed, line up the zero inch (0 cm) mark with your friend's feet again and read the measurement on the yardstick that lines up with the top of the tree.

4. Divide the tree's measurement by your friend's measurement to find out how many times taller the tree is. Now multiply that number by your friend's real height to get the approximate real height of the tree.

5. If you're wondering how long the tree would be if it fell on the ground, just run a tape measure out from the base of the trunk until you've gone the same distance as the tree's height.

Your friend's height on the yardstick: 3" (7.5 cm)

The tree's height on the yardstick: 18" (45 cm)

Your friend's real height: 5' (150 cm)

18 ÷ 3 = 6 or 45 ÷ 7.5 = 6

The tree is six times taller than your friend.

6 x 5' (150 cm) = 30' (9 m), the approximate height of the tree.

HOW FAR?

Farther Than a Grasshopper Hops?

The average everyday garden-variety grasshopper can move about 2½' (75 cm) with each hop. You're thinking, "Big deal," right? Think again! An average grasshopper is only about 1½" (3.75 cm) long. That means it can jump more than 20 times it's length in a single bound! (Beginning to sound more like a SuperHopper now!) Do you think you could match that feat?

Is that Dennis HOPPER?

☆ Try a superhuman hop!

Ask someone to help measure how tall you are. Then, multiply your height by 20 to equal the feat of the grasshopper. Try a running long jump. How far did you go? Now what do you think of that grasshopper's jumping abilities? Bet you'd like a grasshopper or two on your track and field team!

Math Marvel ★

Shrinking Sheep

You know how something that's far away (such as an airplane) can look very tiny, even though we know it's really huge? You can create the same kind of *optical illusion*, which is known as the principle of *diminution* (diminishing or decreasing in size).

☆ Create a sheep ranch!

Cut out several white paper sheep in a variety of sizes. Glue them in place on a sheet of green paper so that the larger ones are along the bottom edge and the smallest is nearer the top. Then, use a black marker to add heads, ears, and legs to your sheep. Doesn't it look like your flock is wandering away? This is what allows artists to create the illusion that certain objects in their drawings are off in the distance.

Measure Your Hand

You can measure string with a ruler, water with a measuring cup, and medicine with a measuring spoon — but how about odd-shaped objects, such as a stone or your hand?

WHAT YOU NEED

Large wide-mouth jar

Shallow baking pan

Water

Measuring cup

WHAT YOU DO

1. Set the jar in the baking pan.

2. Fill the jar to the brim with water.

3. Slowly lower your hand into the jar so that the water comes up to your wrist. Once the water stops flowing out of the jar, remove your hand.

4. Set the jar aside and pour the water from the pan into the measuring cup to find out how many fluid ounces (ml) your hand *displaced* (pushed out of the jar).

5. Multiply the number of ounces by 1.7 — that's the number of cubic inches in a fluid ounce. (For a metric equivalent, multiply by .886 for the answer in cubic centimeters.) Now you know the number of cubic inches (cm) your hand measures!

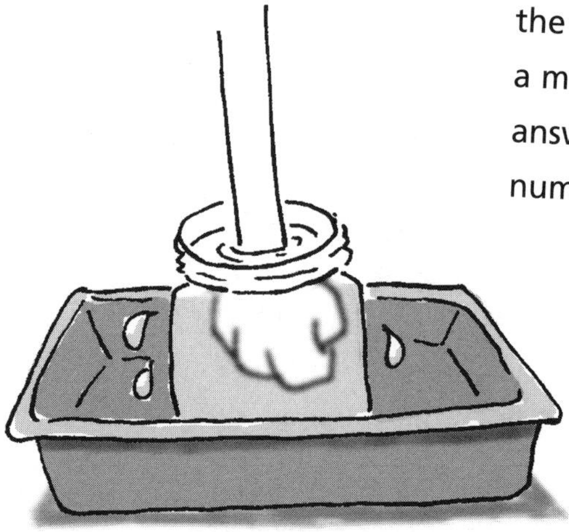

HOW-TO!

Real-world Math™

Where Did the Wood Go?

When you go to a lumberyard to get the wood for your birdhouse (see right), you'll need to ask for two 1X6 ("one by six") pine boards. When you take them home to measure them, however, you'll find that the boards actually measure ³/₄" x 5¹/₂" (2 x 14 cm). "What," you say? That's because lumber is sized according to its original rough cut from the tree, before it is planed and sanded at the sawmill. The planing and sanding reduce the size, so a 1" x 6" (2.5 cm x 15 cm) "rough" board becomes a ³/₄" x 5¹/₂" (2 x 14 cm) finished board — but it's still called a "one by six."

Build a Birdhouse

Imagine baking a cake without a recipe or putting together a model car without directions. There's no telling how things would turn out! The same goes for building a house. That's why carpenters follow *blue-prints* or *plans* — detailed drawings that include the *dimensions* (size) of each room. Here's a set of blueprints you can follow to build a birdhouse. (*NOTE: You can build a lot of really cool things with tools, but handling them is serious business, so never use one without adult supervision!*)

Please?

WHAT YOU NEED

Ruler or carpenter's framing square

Pencil

4' (120 cm) of a 1X6 pine board

Handsaw

Drill with ¹/₈" (2.5 mm) bit and 1¹/₂" (3.8 cm) bit

Galvanized six-penny nails, 16

Hammer

³/₄" (2 cm) exterior-grade plywood, 6¹/₂" x 8¹/₂" (16.25 x 21.25 cm)

Sandpaper, coarse grade

2" (5 cm) brass hinge with screws

Screwdriver

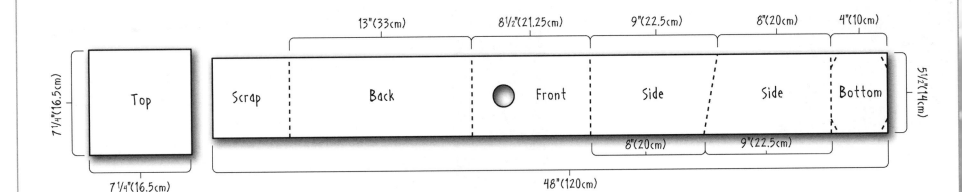

7 1/4"(16.5cm) — Top — 7 1/4"(16.5cm)

Scrap | Back — 13"(33cm) | Front — 8 1/2"(21.25cm) | Side — 9"(22.5cm) | Side — 8"(20cm) | Bottom — 4"(10cm)

8"(20cm)   9"(22.5cm)

48"(120cm)   5 1/2"(14cm)

WHAT YOU DO

1. Measure and mark the pine board as shown; label the pieces.

2. Ask an adult to help you saw the board along the cut lines (particularly the corners of the bottom, which can be tricky but are necessary for drainage). Use the 1 1/2" (3.8 cm) bit to drill the entrance hole in the front.

3. Nail the side pieces to the bottom 1 1/2" (3.8 cm) in from the front and back of each piece. It's easier if you use the 1/8" (2.5 mm) bit to pre-drill holes with help from a grown-up.

4. Center the back piece up against the sides and nail it in place with three nails evenly spaced along each edge. Position the front so that the top edge extends 1/2" (1 cm) above the sides to create a gap for ventilation.

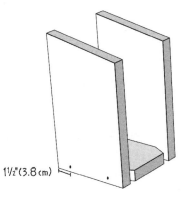

1 1/2"(3.8 cm)

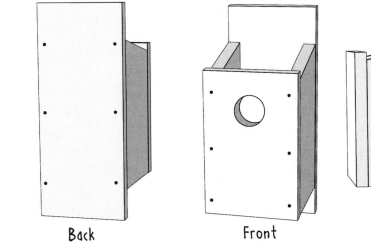

Back   Front   Side

5. Using the hinge, attach the plywood roof to the back. (You may have to sand one of the shorter roof edges first so it will butt up against the back board.)

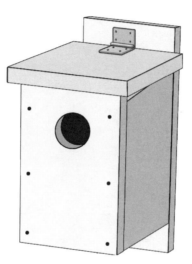

YAY!

Pour Over This!

Suppose you need four cups (1000 ml) of water (not a drop more or less!) to mix up a magic potion. The problem is that you have no measuring cup — just two unmarked containers. You know that one holds exactly five cups (1250 ml) of liquid when it's filled to the brim, and the other holds three cups (750 ml). Can you figure out how to get precisely four cups (1000 ml) of water in one container?

1. Fill the five-cup (1250 ml) container to the brim; then, use it to fill the three-cup (750 ml) container. Now, you should have two cups (500 ml) left in the larger container.

2. Empty the smaller container; then, pour the water that's left in the larger container into the smaller one. Now you have two cups (500 ml) of water in the three-cup (750 ml) container.

3. Refill the larger container and pour enough water from it to bring the level in the three-cup (750 ml) container to the brim. It will take one cup (250 ml) of water. There you are! Now you have exactly four cups (1000 ml) of water in the five-cup (1250 ml) container.

IT'S ABOUT TIME!

Once upon a time, there was no time! Days came and went, but people were too busy looking for food, making clothes, and building shelters to pay as much attention to the passing seasons as we do today. (They simply had no time for it!) Eventually, people started planting food, herding animals, and living in villages. Working together made life easier, and people established a rhythm to their lives. So, for the first time, there was time for time!

Like any newfound treasure, time was suddenly something people kept track of. They invented time-telling devices to measure it to the minute. In fact, the quartz crystal in a modern watch vibrates 100,000 times per second — so regularly that this type of watch is usually not off by more than one second per month!

Take a journey through time, measuring time with a water-drop timer, leaping through calendar years, and going for the gold in backyard Olympic games. Are you ready? There's no time like the present!

I'M...GETTING... VERY...SLEEPY...

12

Grandpa?

61

Make a Water-Drop Timer

Keeping track of time is easy enough when you're wearing a wristwatch, but before 1907, there was no such thing! The electric clock wasn't even invented until 1840. For thousands of years before that, people used such devices as an hourglass filled with sand or a burning candle to tell time. Sometimes they poured water into a bucket with a small hole in the bottom to determine the passage of time based on the amount of water that had leaked out. See if you can tell time with a water clock of your own.

WHAT YOU NEED

Straight pin or thumbtack

Small paper cup

Water

Narrow-mouth jar

Clock or watch with a second hand

WHAT YOU DO

1. Using the pin, make a small hole in the bottom of the cup.

2. Hold the cup over a sink, plugging the hole with your finger while you fill the cup to the brim with water.

3. Hold the cup over the mouth of the jar (it should sit in the lip of the jar, without falling all the way through). Remove your finger, immediately noting the exact time.

You're LATE, there Cowboy!

Good Question!

How did a water timer help if people didn't have clocks to help them know when to start and when to finish measuring the water?

People *gauged* (measured) their water timers against their sun-dials the same way we set electronic devices against our clocks today. The advantage to using a water timer was that once it had begun timing, people could bring the water timer inside and use it to keep time at night or on a cloudy day.

4. Gently (and quickly) set the cup into the jar. When the cup has emptied completely, note the exact time again.

5. Subtract the starting time from the ending time to find out precisely how long it took for your water clock to run dry.

Drifting Off

It takes the average person seven minutes to fall asleep.

Use your cup to tell the next few hours of time. You may be pretty busy, though! If it takes 30 minutes for your full cup of water to empty out, how many times will you have to fill it over a three-hour period? Compare your answer with the one at the bottom of the page.

Water-Drop Timer: You'll have to fill it six times — once every half hour for three hours.

Backyard Olympics

Keep close track of the time (using a stopwatch if you have one) with this roster of games you can organize for a day of fun in your neighborhood. In each event, award three points to the winner, two points to the player who comes in second, and one point for the third-place competitor. At the end of the day, tally everyone's points to find out who wins the gold, silver, or bronze.

FEATHER WEIGHT LIFT

One at a time, have contestants try to keep a feather aloft for as long as possible by blowing under it. The clock starts the instant the contestant releases the feather.

MAD DASH DRIBBLE

Set a lawn chair at the far end of your driveway or walkway. One at a time, have competitors dribble a basketball from the starting line, around the chair, and back.

Keeping Score

To keep track of how they're doing, the athletes at your backyard Olympics will need scorecards. To make them, divide index cards into four columns labeled: *Event, Time, Distance,* and *Points Scored.*

EVENT	TIME	Distance	Points Scored
Feather Weight Lift			
Mad Dash Dribble			
Sand Can Slalom			
Popcorn Pitch			

SAND CAN SLALOM

Fill empty cans with sand or pebbles to weigh them down. Arrange them in a line, spaced 8' (240 cm) apart. Have competitors walk as fast they can (runners are disqualified) from start to finish, weaving around the cans as they go.

POPCORN PITCH

You'll need a pile of popcorn for this event! Have players compete to see who can pitch popped kernels (one at a time) as far as possible in 30 seconds.

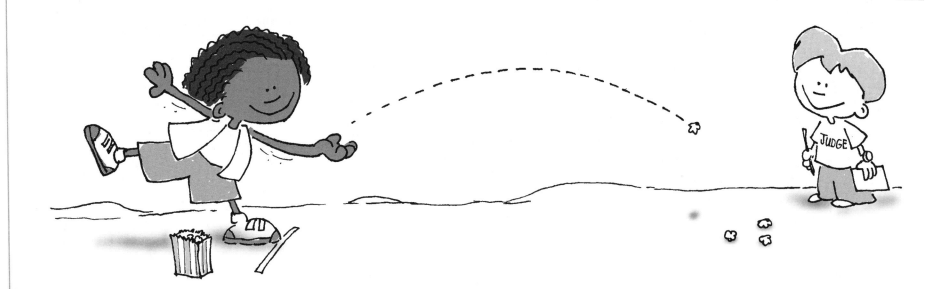

Fancy Footwork

When professional skaters go into one of those dazzling spins on ice, they sometimes complete up to nine *revolutions* (turns) per second! Wow! I wonder how they don't get dizzy!

Gertrude Caroline Ederle was still a teenager in 1926 when she became the first woman to swim 35 miles (56 km) across the English Channel from France to England. Her time of 14 hours and 31 minutes broke the men's record by nearly two hours! Way to go, Gertrude!

Math Marvel ★

A Split Second

Olympic athletes can be so evenly
matched that their times need to be
measured in tenths of a second! To get
an idea of how incredibly fast that is,
keep an eye on the second hand of your
watch while you try counting to 10 in
one second! That's right — *one second!*

Math Marvel ★

Catch a Dollar Bill on the Fly

Ask a friend to form a V with her index
and middle fingers. Hold out a dollar bill so
that the middle of the bill is between her
two fingers and challenge her to grasp the
bill once you drop it. Almost certainly, the
dollar will slip through her fingers. That's
because it takes the average person two-
tenths of a second to react to something she
sees. In that short time, the dollar bill will
have already fallen a few inches (cm)
below your friend's hand!

TIME ZONES

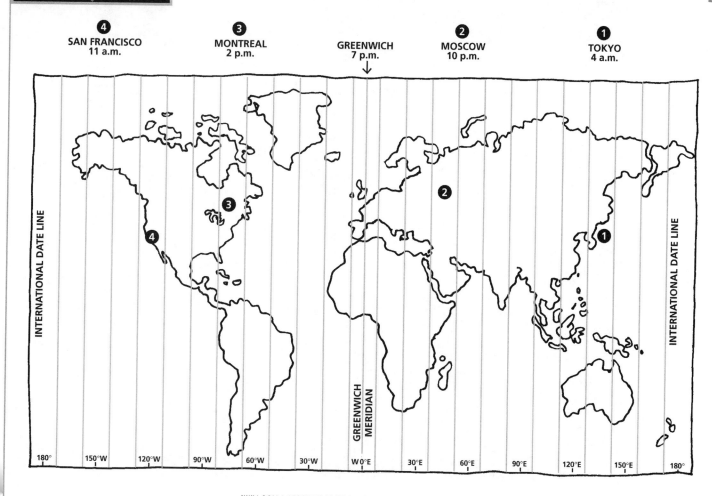

WHAT IN THE WORLD?

If you look at a world map, you'll see a grid of imaginary lines running up and down (meridians, or longitude lines) and across (parallels, or latitude lines). Earth is a sphere with 360°, and these meridians and parallels measure off these degrees around the globe. See if you can find the meridian marked 0° that connects the North and South Poles. That line is the *Grand Meridian*, and it is actually marked on the ground at Greenwich, England.

Time on the Web

For a very cool website on world time zones, check out <www.worldtimezone.com>.

④ SAN FRANCISCO
11 a.m.

③ MONTREAL
2 p.m.

GREENWICH
7 p.m.
↓

② MOSCOW
10 p.m.

① TOKYO
4 a.m.

For every 15° east of the Grand Meridian, the time is one hour ahead of Greenwich time; for every 15° west of Greenwich, the time is one hour *behind*. That adds up to 24 different time zones around the world! Look at the map again. Suppose it's 7:00 P.M. in Greenwich. Can you figure out what time it would be in Tokyo, Japan? How about Moscow, Russia? Or Montreal in Canada? San Francisco in the U.S.? Find the answers below.

INTERNATIONAL DATE LINE

INTERNATIONAL DATE LINE

GREENWICH MERIDIAN

180° 150°W 120°W 90°W 60°W 30°W 0°E 30°E 60°E 90°E 120°E 150°E 180°

Time Zones: Tokyo: 4:00 A.M.   Moscow: 10:00 P.M.   Montreal: 2:00 P.M.   San Francisco: 11:00 A.M.

GIVE EARTH A SPIN

When our planet was young and a mass of dust and rock about 4.6 billion years ago, it was spinning at about 4,000 mph (6,436 kph). Today it rotates at about one-quarter of that speed. And it's slowing down all the time partly because of the effects of our sloshing oceans.

☆ An eggs-ellent eggs-periment!

To see what a drag all that liquid can be, spin a hardboiled egg and a raw egg at the same time on a countertop. Watch what happens. Then, compare your results with those described at the bottom of the page.

How Close Is That Storm?

We all — including athletes playing ball and backyard Olympians — know to get inside as soon as we hear a clap of thunder or see a flash of lightning. Light travels through air faster than anything else we know of in the universe, so the next time it's lightning and thundering outside, you can figure out how far away the storm is — and whether it's moving closer or farther away.

☆ Quick as a flash!

Find a clock or watch with a second hand. As soon as you see a flash of lightning, start watching the second hand to keep track of how much time passes before you hear the crack of thunder. Divide the number of seconds by five. Your answer will tell you how many miles away the storm is. Figure the time between the next few lightning flashes and thunderclaps. If the moments between the lightning and thunder grow shorter, the storm is getting nearer; longer, and it's moving away.

An eggs-ellent eggs-periment!: The solid egg spins faster and longer, while the raw egg quickly slows down to a halt because the liquid inside, like the oceans on Earth, slows it down.

TIME MARCHES ON

Time is one of those concepts difficult for humans to understand. After all, we can't see it, touch it, taste it, smell it, or hear it. No wonder we have such a hard time grasping its meaning!

Have you ever heard the saying, "Time flies when you're having fun?" Well, it's true, isn't it? Think about your favorite activity at school; it sure goes by faster than your least favorite activity; yet, a clock or a calendar counts them exactly the same. There are other expressions for time, too, such as "Time marches on." Try to imagine what someone was thinking the first time he used one of these expressions. Then, draw the picture that comes to your mind.

When Do Years Leap?

Deciding exactly how many days would make up a year was no easy matter. In fact, it took centuries! The Egyptians got the ball rolling more than 6,000 years ago by choosing 365, about one-quarter (¼ or .25) day less than Earth's revolution around the sun. But those quarter-days eventually added up: In time, summer celebrations were falling in the middle of winter! That's when the Romans came up with the idea in 47 B.C. of adding an extra day every fourth year (leap year). But that added up to 11 extra minutes, and guess what — eventually winter holidays were being celebrated in the summer.

Finally, the Gregorian calendar (the one we use today) was created in 1582. Every fourth year is still a leap year (with an extra day, February 29), except if the year is divisible by 100 (such as 1900 or 2100). However, if it's divisible by both 100 and 400 (such as the year 2000 or 2400), then it is a leap year! Whew! This mathematical formula solved the 11-minute problem and keeps us on time all the time!

✰ List the leaps!

Can you guess how many leap years will occur during this millennium — between the years 2000 and 3000? Try to list them all; then compare your list with the one on the next page.

A Baffling Birthday

How old would someone born in 2002 B.C. be in 1990 B.C.?

24 leap years in all!

2004	2028	2052	2076
2008	2032	2056	2080
2012	2036	2060	2084
2016	2040	2064	2088
2020	2044	2068	2092
2024	2048	2072	2096

Baffling Birthday: Not old at all. The person wouldn't even be born yet!

WHAT ARE B.C. AND A.D.?

When our calendar was invented, Christianity was not only a religion, it was also a government. The people who established our calendar divided history into two time periods — the years before Christ was born and the years after Christ was born.

The years after Christ's birth were written as A.D., an abbreviation for the Latin words that meant "in the year of the Lord." These years start from the year 1 and move upward, so the year 2001 comes *after* the year 2000.

The years before Christ was born are written as B.C. ("before Christ"), and these numbers work in the opposite way. They start from large numbers way back at the beginning of time and work their way down to the more recent years. In B.C. years, the year 2001 comes *before* the year 2000.

Since many people in the world practice religions other than Chrisitianity, someone decided to use more neutral terms than "before Christ" and "year of the Lord." The practice caught on, so now you may see the term B.C.E. instead of B.C. and C.E. instead of A.D. These terms mean "before the common era" and "common era."

Save That Date

Here's a calendar you never have to throw away because the days of each month are numbered, not named. That makes it a perfect calendar for recording friends' and relatives' birthdays, anniversaries, and other special occasions that happen every year. It's called a *perpetual calendar* because it can be used year in and year out.

WHAT YOU NEED

8¹/₂" x 14" (21 x 35 cm) plain paper

Ruler

Pencil

Colored markers or crayons

Stickers (optional)

Hole punch

Ribbon

WHAT YOU DO

1. Count out 12 sheets of paper and lay them on your worktable with the short ends on the top and bottom. Use the top quarter of the page to print the name of the month. Draw a picture or design to go with it, use stickers to decorate, or write the month in *calligraphy* (fancy handwriting).

2. On the lower portion, draw a numbered line for each day in the month. (Don't forget to give February 29 days, even though leap year only rolls around every four years.)

3. Punch matching holes at the top of each page as shown; then, bind the pages together in calendar order with ribbon.

4. Fill in the calendar by writing various occasions on the appropriate lines. If you want to keep track of a person's age, just include the year she was born beside the occasion.

January

16 Theresa's B-DAY 1984

1	17
2	18
3	19
4	20
5	21
6	22
7	23 MOM & DAD'S ANNIVERSARY
8	24
9	25
10	26
11	27
12	28
13	29
14	30
15	31

Months in Your Hand

Make a fist of your left hand and pretend that the four knuckles at the base of your fingers are mountains and the spaces between them are valleys. Now walk the index finger of your right hand across the mountains and valleys, naming the months and how many days they have as you go ("January, 31," for example). When you get to the fourth knuckle, switch hands and continue with the first knuckle of your right hand. Notice any pattern? The months that fall on the mountains have 31 days and the ones in a valley have 30 (except February, which has 28, except when leap year gives it an extra day). Where does your birthday month fall — on a mountain or in a valley? How about the birthday months of your friends and family members?

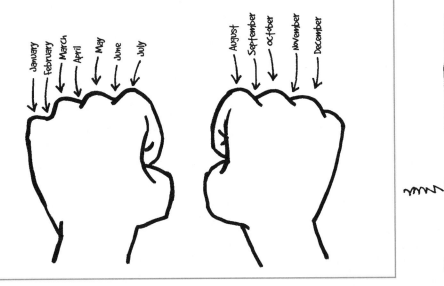

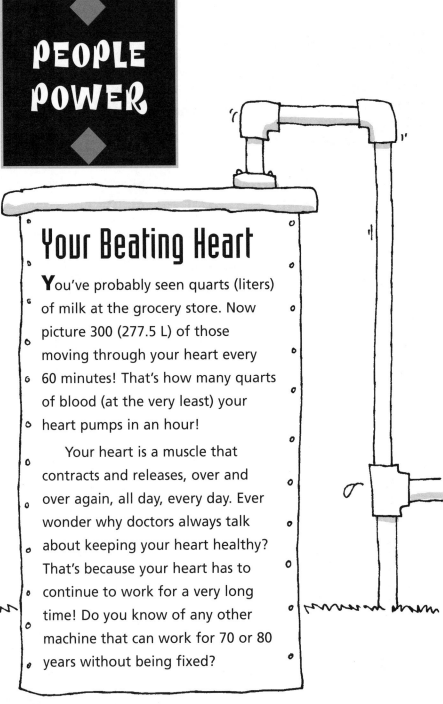

PEOPLE POWER

Your Beating Heart

You've probably seen quarts (liters) of milk at the grocery store. Now picture 300 (277.5 L) of those moving through your heart every 60 minutes! That's how many quarts of blood (at the very least) your heart pumps in an hour!

Your heart is a muscle that contracts and releases, over and over again, all day, every day. Ever wonder why doctors always talk about keeping your heart healthy? That's because your heart has to continue to work for a very long time! Do you know of any other machine that can work for 70 or 80 years without being fixed?

Pumping Power

Do you know how hard your heart works? Find out by making a few calculations.

1. Use your fingertips to locate a pulse beat in your wrist or neck.

2. Use a watch or clock with a second hand to count the beats for one minute. Do this twice while you are relaxing and twice just after riding your bike, playing with your dog, or racing up the stairs.

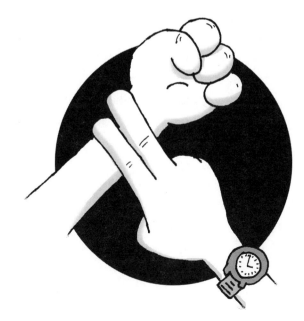

3. Add up the four pulse readings and divide by four to find your *average pulse rate per minute*.

4. Multiply your average by 60 (number of minutes per hour) to get the number of beats per hour. Then, multiply that number by 24 to see how your heartbeat compares to the average adult rate of 100,000 times a day! Whew! And just think — your heart can't take a day off — ever!

Math Marvel ★

★

The Speed of a Sneeze

Have you ever tried to hold back a sneeze? If so, you probably know it's nearly impossible. When dust irritates the nerve endings in your nose, your body takes a deep breath and closes your windpipe. This causes pressure to build up in your lungs. When your windpipe opens up again, air blasts the dust out of your nose at nearly 100 mph (160.9 kph)!

Bless you.

Hearty Hearts

The Grinch's heart may have "grown" when he became more caring, but in the real world the size of a heart has a lot to do with how hard it has to work. Bigger animals, with larger hearts, have much slower pulse rates than tiny critters. An elephant's heart, for example, beats between 20 to 30 times per minute. That's downright leisurely compared with a mouse's heart, which pumps more than 480 times per minute!

Did you see a pair of khakis go flying by just now?

How Probable Is It?

Suppose your cousin, who lives out of state, e-mails you an average of three to four times a week. It's Wednesday night, and you haven't heard from him since Sunday. Do you think you'll get an e-mail message today? Based on his past pattern, it's reasonable to predict that you will.

Mathematicians and scientists use *statistics* (data they've collected over time) to figure out whether the likelihood of a certain event happening again is favorable (it will happen) or unfavorable (it won't happen). Is a certain baseball player likely to hit the ball when he's up at bat? (Just look at his stats!) Is the probability of rain high today? (What's the usual weather pattern?) Knowing what "the odds are" (see page 91) can make a difference in your planning. You probably wouldn't call off a family picnic if there were a 20 percent chance of rain, but a 90 percent chance might make you reconsider. And still, in either case, it might or might not rain, because even if something probably will happen, it is not definite! (Take your cousin's e-mail, for instance: What if his hard drive has crashed or his Internet service provider isn't working? Then you won't get that e-mail, even though you predicted it was likely you would.) When trying to make predictions based on probability, you just never know for sure.

Go Fish!

UNDERSTANDING PERCENTAGES

When we talk about percentages, we use 100 to mean "all." For example, if you ate 100 percent of your dinner, you ate all of it. Say you didn't like dinner, and your mom said, "Eat half, and then you may be excused." If you did as she suggested, you would have eaten 50 percent of your dinner (since half of 100 is 50). So, when something has a *20 percent chance* of happening, it means that out of the last 100 times when everything about the situation was the same, that particular outcome happened 20 times.

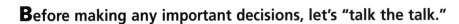

Before making any important decisions, let's "talk the talk."

P R O B A B I L I T Y is the likelihood that something will occur.

This can be described in *whole numbers* (for example, a 1-in-5 chance) or in *percentages* (a .20 or 20 percent chance).

A 1-in-5 chance and a 20 percent chance are the same *odds*. You are saying that out of five chances, you are likely to do something one time.

Say, for example, you have soccer practice after school this week Monday through Thursday. Friday you plan to go straight home after school. The probability that you'll get home before 3:30 this week is 1-*in*-5 (one out of a total of five).

Chancy Lingo

ODDS compare your chances *for* and *against* something by stating the number of times something will happen compared with the times it won't. For example, if the *probability* of something happening is 1-*in*-5, the *odds* would be 1-*to*-4 in favor of it happening, or 4-*to*-1 *against* it happening.

Take that soccer practice: The odds of your getting home before 3:30 this week are 1-*to*-4 (one day it's likely you'll get home early; four days it's not likely). Expressed another way, the odds are 4-*to*-1 that you won't make it home early (it's unlikely on four days and likely on only one).

FAVORED
OUTCOME

50:50 or *50-50* means that out of 100 times when something happens, it may result in one outcome 50 times and a different outcome the other 50 times. It indicates that half of the time you'll get one result, and the other half you'll get the other result. So, what does 30:70 mean?

A **PREDICTION** is an "educated" guess — based on all of the information you have — about what the result will be.

A **FAVORED** outcome is the one that has the best chance of happening, or the best odds.

A **LONG SHOT** is an outcome that is unlikely to happen, though it is still possible.

Numbers Count

Every 10 years, the U.S. Census Bureau sends out questionnaires for households to fill out and mail back. While names and personal information are kept confidential, general answers — how many people live in your house, how old they are, whether or not you have a pet — are compiled and made available to all kinds of organizations and businesses.

These statistics help determine which communities need more services — everything from hospitals (based on the number of elderly people in a community) and schools (based on the number of school-age children in a community) to roadways and airports. How do you suppose McDonald's or Burger King decides where to build its restaurants?

Chance of Rain

Twice a day, the National Weather Service and other weather services around the world send up helium balloons equipped to measure the wind, temperature, and *humidity* (how much moisture is in the air). All of that information is put into a computer and compared with past statistics so that meteorologists can tell us the probability of rain that day.

If you hear there's a 40 percent chance of rain, it means that out of the last 100 times when the weather conditions were similar to the current weather, it rained 40 times. Are you going to chance it and go to the beach anyway?

Figure Out Your Batting Average

Here's how you can figure out your hitting average. Don't be surprised if it tops the pros — Little League players have been known to have batting averages as high as .800! All you need is a baseball or softball and bat, and a couple of friends to pitch and umpire.

1. Have someone pitch to you several times "at bat" — that is, until you either strike out (miss three pitches) or get to base by hitting the ball. Keep track of the number of times at bat. (Your first time at bat, for example, you might miss the first pitch and then hit the ball into left field, getting to first base. This would count as one time at bat even though you received two pitches. Your second time at bat, you might hit a foul ball and then strike out. All four pitches would be your second time at bat.)

2. Add up the times you earned a base by successfully hitting the ball. (Fouls don't count, and neither do walks because the base wasn't earned by hitting the ball.)

Times you hit the ball	3
Divided by times up at bat	5
$3 \div 5 = .600$	
Your baseball average	.600 = 600

So, slightly more than half the time you step up to bat, you get a hit. Way to go!

3. Divide the number of successful times at bat (when you earned a base by hitting the ball) by the number of times at bat; then move the decimal point three places to the right. (Say you came up with .600, for example. You would say, "My average is six hundred" or "I bat six hundred.")

An Average Average?

If you want to know how good a batter your favorite baseball player is, look up his batting average to find out how many times he hit the ball compared with the number of times he was up at bat. If it's close to .300, he's considered really good; .350, and he's terrific!

KIDS CAN!

During the 1992 Dixie Youth Baseball World Series for 6- to 8-year-old players, Jacob Gillespie of Texarkana South, Texas, ended up with a .750 batting average!

And now batting... JACOB GILLESPIE!

Uh oh!

GAMES OF CHANCE

Whenever you don't know the answer to a question and you have two choices — for example, whether something's true or false, or which of two forks in the road will lead you to your destination — you have a 50-50 chance of choosing correctly. Not too reassuring, is it? You can always better your chances of success by studying up on the matter (say, by referring to a map when you reach a fork in the road), but sometimes — when you're playing a game, for instance — having a 50-50 chance can be more exciting because at even odds, the outcome is hardest to predict.

◆ IT'S A TOSS-UP: FLIPPING PENNIES

You've seen it at the beginning of many sports games — a couple of players from each team meet in center field, where an official tosses a coin to see who will start with the ball. Because the odds of getting what you call (heads or tails) are equal (a coin can only land on one of two sides) this tradition is accepted as a fair way to decide. If you were on a team that always chose heads, how do you think you'd make out in the long run? Let's find out!

1. Print the numbers 1 through 5 down the left margin of a piece of paper.

2. Flip a coin into the air 10 times. Next to number 1, write down the number of times it lands on heads. Then, complete four more sets of 10 tosses and record the results next to numbers 2 through 5.

3. Now divide each recorded number by 10 to figure out what percent of the time heads landed up in each set. (You beat the odds every time you scored more than 50 percent!)

GOOD LUCK!

Let's say the following results come up in all of the tosses:

Number of times heads comes up in 10 coin tosses

1. **7**   7 ÷ 10 = .70 or 70 percent for the first set of 10
2. **5**   5 ÷ 10 = .50 or 50 percent for the second set of 10
3. **4**   4 ÷ 10 = .40 or 40 percent for the third set of 10
4. **3**   3 ÷ 10 = .30 or 30 percent for the fourth set of 10
5. **6**   6 ÷ 10 = .60 or 60 percent for the fifth set of 10

4. Want to figure out how all of the tosses fared when the results are combined? Simply add up the number of tosses that resulted in heads within each round. Divide the total by 50 (your total number of tosses). Did the results beat the odds?

7 + 5 + 4 + 3 + 6 = 25

25 ÷ 50 = .50 or 50 percent

Now try it yourself. How many of your tosses landed heads-up? What percentages did you get? Did your percentages beat the odds?

◆ ROCK, PAPER, SCISSORS ◆

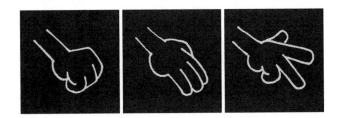

Winning this game for two is purely a matter of chance because even though certain symbols triumph over others, none triumphs over all; and no one ever knows which symbol the other player will decide to use. For a fun twist, try playing this game step by step, the way kids in China do.

Sit side by side on the bottom step of a short staircase. On the count of three, both players bring one hand forward in the symbol of a rock (a fist), paper (four fingers held straight out), or scissors (two fingers forming a V). The player with the winning symbol (paper covers rock, rock breaks scissors, and scissors cut paper) moves up one step. Keep playing until someone reaches the top step to win the game. Play to the top step four times, noting who wins each time. Did it come out to 50-50?

◆ ELIMINATION ◆

Here's another game in which strategy won't help you. It's all a matter of probabilities and chance, along with lots of shakes, rattles, and rolls!

Gather a number of friends and a pair of dice. Have each player write down numbers 2 through 12 on a slip of paper. Now take turns rolling the dice. After each roll, add the two numbers that are showing; then, cross the sum off your list. The first player to eliminate all the numbers on his paper wins.

BEATING THE ODDS

(Or the Odds Beating You!)

When you buy a raffle ticket at a school fundraiser and your number isn't picked, you're still a winner because you've donated to a worthwhile cause. If you buy a lottery ticket, on the other hand, it's practically a sure bet that all you'll end up with is a lighter wallet!

Here's why: Suppose you're buying a ticket that requires you to pick six numbers from 1 to 49 that have to be in the right order to win. The probability that you'll do so is 1-in-10 billion! Even if the order of the numbers didn't matter, your chances would be very slim: 1-in-14 million. Just think: If you bought seven million tickets, you'd still only have a 50-50 chance of winning — and you'd be out a few million dollars for the price of the tickets. That's why the lottery is good business — for the people running it, that is — *not* for the players.

Have you ever wondered what makes a person blond or brunette, tall or short, freckled or not? Each of us inherited thousands of genes that spelled out exactly what we would look like. Take your eye color, for example. It was determined by two genes: one from your mother and the other from your father. If both of those genes were brown, then your eyes are brown. If one gene was brown and one gene was blue, then your eyes are still brown because the brown-color gene is *dominant* over the blue-color gene. (That means it's stronger than the blue-color gene and always wins out.) In order to inherit blue eyes, *both* parents would have needed to contribute a blue-color gene.

The Better to See You With

Here's how you can figure out what the odds are of being born with a particular eye color, a method that was determined by Gregor Mendel in the 1800s.

BROWN-EYED MOM

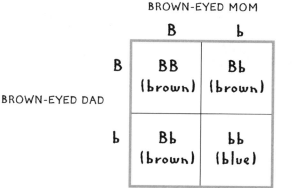

	B	b
B	BB (brown)	Bb (brown)
b	Bb (brown)	bb (blue)

BROWN-EYED DAD

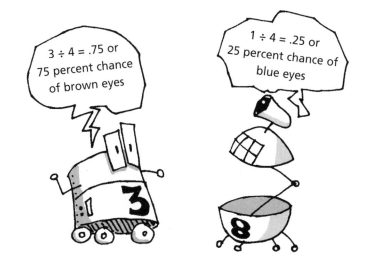

3 ÷ 4 = .75 or 75 percent chance of brown eyes

1 ÷ 4 = .25 or 25 percent chance of blue eyes

WHAT YOU NEED

Paper and pencil

Calculator

Let's do it!

WHAT YOU DO

1. Draw a square and divide it in half vertically and horizontally to create four equal-sized boxes. This is called a Mendel box.

2. Suppose each of your parents has one gene for brown eye color (written as capital B because it's dominant) and one for blue (a lowercase b). These gene pairs are written Bb x Bb. Print one gene combination across the top of the box and the other down the left side.

3. Figure out the four combinations you could inherit by pairing each of the genes on the left with a gene at the top; then write the pairs in the appropriate box. (Note: If the dominant gene for brown (B) shows up in a pair, it is always printed first.)

Since brown shows up in three possible combinations (2 for Bb and 1 for BB), the probability of having brown eyes is 3-in-4, or 75 percent. That leaves a 1-in-4 (or 25 percent) probability of inheriting the bb combination for blue eyes.

☆ Which B will you be?

Using the Mendel box, figure out your probabilities with these "parent genes":

BB x bb   BB x Bb   Bb x bb

Imaginary Menagerie

Now that you know how genes determine the physical traits we have, can you predict what would happen if you were to cross a Whooflelump with a Snozopolus?

Here is one example to get you started, using two gene traits from the key: G for giant feet and d for dainty feet.

	G	d
d	Gd	dd
d	Gd	dd

Gd = 2; dd = 2

So, the offspring has a 50-50 chance of getting dainty or giant hooves.

Now, create more combinations and drawings for an imaginary menagerie of incredible creatures!

GENE KEY

Giant hooves (G) or dainty hooves (d)

Polka-dot fur (P) or striped fur (s)

Long and wrinkly trunk (L) or cute-as-a-button nose (b)

Fluffy tail (F) or curly tail (c)

Whooflelump gene pairs: Gd, ss, LL, Fc

Snozopolus gene pairs: dd, PP, Lb, Fc

★ **Make some crazy critters!**

Check out the gene key on page 102 (dominant genes are capitalized). Then, look next to each critter's name to find out what pairs of genes it has. Using the same Mendel-box method, determine what gene combinations could be passed on. Then, draw a picture of what their imaginary children might look like. Remember: There are a number of possibilities!

MONEY MATH

Suppose your family is participating in a neighborhood tag sale, and someone offers you two dried codfish for your old catcher's mitt. Either he's pulling your leg, or there's a slim chance — OK, a super-slim chance — that he's a Norwegian who's traveled forward in time. (Or, he could be from Portugal, where dried codfish is a popular food!) Thousands of years ago, people traded lots of different things (from drums and eggs to hoes and kettles) for other items they needed or wanted. It was called *bartering*.

Over the years, money has had more than a few make-overs. Even the bills and coins in our pockets can look a bit old-fashioned next to the colorful plastic debit cards that people use at supermarkets these days. But no matter what forms of money we use, they all have one thing in common — they enable us to buy what we need, as well as share what we have with people who don't have as much. Here's a wealth of tips on how you can earn it and double it, passing the wealth around!

YAY!

Throw in a sardine and we've got a deal.

DOLLARS & CENTS

If you think that $1.00 is always worth 100¢, well, you're right — technically speaking, that is. You see, the *value* of that $1.00 — meaning what that $1.00 will buy — is constantly changing, depending on *where* you are, *what* you are buying, and *when* you are buying it.

Confused yet? Well, so are most of us when it comes to sizing up what something is "worth."

Money Monikers

What's a *moniker*? It's a nickname. And it just so happens that money has plenty of monikers that turn up in everyday conversation:

Cold, hard cash

Dough

Moola

Scratch

Loot

Bucks

Perhaps folks in your area use nicknames that aren't included here. Listen to conversations around your home, school, and neighborhood to see how many money monikers you can add to this list.

Sure, I'll do your homework. But it will cost you a fin.

HOW MUCH IS YOUR DOLLAR WORTH?

In the early 1960s, you could buy a loaf of bread for a quarter. And gasoline cost about 35¢ a gallon — that means that you could fill a tank, even a big tank, for about $5!

What's up these days? Prices are! It's called *inflation*. Every year the price of goods and services seems to rise about 3 percent — that's three cents for every dollar. Ask your parents or grandparents how much allowance or spending money they earned when they were kids. How does it compare with what you earn today? Or ask how much they earned baby-sitting. In the '60s, most kids earned $1.00 an hour. In some parts of the country today, kids can earn up to $10 an hour! That's about a 37 percent increase every year. Not bad compared with the standard rate of inflation at 3 percent! What do you think might explain the fact that babysitting prices rose much higher than other prices?

★ "When I was a kid,..."

So do your parents give you a better allowance than they received? Let's add it up.

Suppose you get $5 to $7 a week for helping out with the household chores. What would you think if your parents told you that, when they were your age, their allowance ranged from 50¢ to 75¢ a week? That's just a fraction — one tenth, to be exact — of yours! Does that mean you can buy 10 times more than your parents could? Not necessarily.

Make a short list of things you can buy with your allowance, such as a movie ticket, a couple of magazines, or two ice-cream sundaes. Now ask your parents what those same items cost when they were kids, and you'll find the prices were a lot lower. In fact, your parents probably spent between 50¢ and 75¢ for a movie ticket — about one-tenth of what it costs now! Things have gotten more expensive, so kids have about as much buying power today as they did back then.

TANK OF GAS 1962: $5

TANK OF GAS TODAY: $25.00

LOAF OF BREAD 1962: 25¢

LOAF OF BREAD TODAY: $1.50

1 WEEK ALLOWANCE 1962: 75¢

1 WEEK ALLOWANCE TODAY: $7.00

PORTABLE CD PLAYER 1962:

Hey, Wait a minute...

3

The Money Shredders

Believe it or not, even money is recycled. Every day, the 12 U.S. Federal Reserve Banks destroy millions of "spent" bills (we're talking worn-out bills!). While plenty of those shredded dollars end up in landfills, some are used to make insulation and various paper products, such as stationery. Just think, that last letter you mailed to your pen pal may have been written on a recycled $100 bill!

INFLATED CASH!

How is it possible for the price of a hamburger to change so much? It's because of inflation, which means a rise in prices over a span of time.

It works like this: Say that you have $10 each week for lunch money, and the school lunch costs $2. You could afford to buy lunch each day of the week.

But what happens when the cost of lunch goes up to $3, and your lunch money is raised to only $12? You'll be out of lunch money after only four days, so you'll have to bring your lunch on Friday.

With fewer kids eating school lunches, the people who make the lunches won't be making enough money, so they may raise the price again to $4 a day. When that happens, you'll be able to buy lunch only three days out of the five days.

The result of inflation, then, is that over time, we can buy less with the same amount of money. So it seems as if our money is worth less.

LUNCH MONEY=$10
LUNCH COST=$2

LUNCH MONEY=$12
LUNCH COST=$3

LUNCH MONEY=$12
LUNCH COST=$4

Moola for the Movies

And it isn't all about dollars and cents. A lot of money talk has to do with what one country's money is worth compared with another country's money. Yes, it's a *global economy*. Let's suppose there are four exchange students (from France, Germany, Great Britain, and Italy) going to your school. They really want to see an American film on the big screen. The manager of the local theater is willing to discount the ticket prices to $3 each. Using the exchange rates listed, can you help each student figure out what the admission price would be equivalent to in her country's currency? Compare your answers with the ones at the bottom of the page.

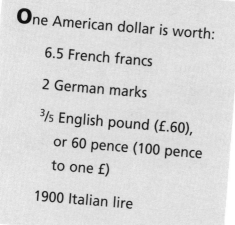

One American dollar is worth:

6.5 French francs

2 German marks

3/5 English pound (£.60), or 60 pence (100 pence to one £)

1900 Italian lire

I only have $5, but you have 3800 Lire!

500,000 Lire (Italy)

5 Pounds (England)

50 Marks (Germany)

20 Francs (France)

Movie Moola: 19.5 francs, 6 marks, 14/5 £ (£1.80), 5700 lira

TIPPING TIPS

The last time you went out to eat, did you wonder why the person who paid the bill "tipped" the server? In the restaurant business, owners pay their servers a very low hourly wage; servers earn the rest of their salaries from the tips they receive from customers. Assuming your food is great and the server is friendly and attentive, how big a tip should you leave? Generally, a tip for good service is 15 to 20 percent of the check total (before you add the tax), depending on the custom where you live. But if you are out for a snack at a kid-friendly place, and you don't sit there for hours, 10 percent is fine.

☆ "Uh-oh! I just ate the tip!"

You're planning to treat your friend to a snack before the two of you go to the movies. You already know you're going to get the grilled cheese sandwich and a vanilla milkshake and that he's going to have a meatball sub and a large soda (you've eaten there before), so you know the bill is going to be the same as it always is: $9.25 with 55¢ tax. You have $10.00 in your pocket for the snacks. How much more will you need in order to leave a reasonable tip? After you've figured it out, compare your answer to the one at the bottom of the page.

Plan ahead!: $9.25 x .10 = 93¢ for the tip, plus 55¢ for tax, comes to $10.73. With only $10 in your pocket, you would need 73¢ more.

MONEY TALKS

What does it say? Hit the jackpot by matching up the following financial phrases with the right meanings. Remember to jot your answers on a scrap of paper, not in the book!

1. Tighter than the bark on a tree
2. Bottom dollar
3. Chicken feed
4. Too much candy for the penny
5. Pony up
6. Burn a hole in your pocket
7. In the red
8. Nest egg
9. In the black
10. For a song
11. Raking it in

a. Profitable, having made money
b. Very inexpensive
c. Unprofitable, owing money
d. A deal that's too good to be true
e. Money that gets spent very quickly
f. Cheap, miserly
g. Your last dollar
h. Small change, not a lot of money
i. Money that's been put away as savings
j. To pay
k. Earning a lot of money

Denim Dollars

The paper on which U.S. money is printed is made with a secret formula that contains denim — just like your jeans!

CHICKEN FEED ATM

5⁰⁰   50⁰⁰
10⁰⁰   50⁰⁰
20⁰⁰ 100⁰⁰

Money Talks: 1. f; 2. g; 3. h; 4. d; 5. j; 6. e; 7. c; 8. i; 9. a; 10. b; 11. k.

111

Money Math

Furry-Friend Finances

If you have a pet, there's no doubt you think it's worth every penny your family spends on it. Exactly how many pennies do you think that adds up to, anyway? Make some estimates about how much money is spent for your pet in one year for the items listed. Then, make a budget. Track your family's actual pet costs, do some research on the World Wide Web, and call your local pet store and veterinary office to determine the real costs. So even if you work every weekend, can you pay Fido's bills?

1. List all the things your pet needs in a year, starting with chow. Suppose your dog (or cat or gerbil) eats 10 ounces (250 g) of food a day. Multiply that by 365 to see how many ounces (grams) he eats in a year; then divide your answer by 16 ounces (.45 kg) to get the total number of pounds (kg). If a bag of food that weighs 20 pounds (9 kg) costs $16, figure out how much a year's supply of food would cost.

Substitute the number of ounces your pet really eats per day and the cost for a 20-pound bag to get an accurate cost for your pet.

10 ounces (280 g) x 365 days = 3,650 ounces per year (102,200 g)

3,650 ounces per year (102,200 g) ÷ 16 ounces per pound (1,000 g per kg) = 228 pounds per year (102.2kg)

228 pounds per year (102.2 kg) ÷ 20 pounds per bag (9 kg) = 11.4 bags per year (Let's call it 12.)

12 bags x $16 = $192

Real-World Math

2. Add all the other items your pet needs or uses.

Expenses

	Estimated Cost (per year)	Actual Cost (per year)
Treats	___	___
Toys	___	___
Annual health care *(shots, teeth cleaning, vitamins, etc.)*	___	___
Flea and tick prevention	___	___
A collar and leash	___	___
Bed	___	___
Town license	___	___
Kennel fees or pet-care fees when you go on vacation	___	___
Grooming *(nail clippings, shampoo, brushes, skunk spray, etc.)*	___	___
Emergency medical fund *(surgery, sedation, anesthesia, hospitalization, antibiotics, X-rays, etc.)*	___	___
Total Annual Budget *(excluding food)*	___	___

How close were your estimates? Will the money you earn mowing lawns and babysitting cover the costs of maintaining your pet? If you really want to find out how hard it is to stay on a budget, ask your family members to save the receipts (set up a labeled box, "Fido's Expenses," where receipts can be left) for all of the money they spend on your pet. Add them up at the end of the year. Did you stay within the final figure, or did you go over your budget?

KID BIZ

No need to wait until you're an adult to start a business. With a little planning, you can be "raking in" some hard-earned cash. You'll see — money earned from hard work seems to be a lot more valuable!

POTENTIAL KID BUSINESSES

Basically there are two different types of businesses kids can start: ones that provide a *service* (such as mowing lawns) and ones that sell *goods* (such as handmade pies or T-shirts). Here are a few ideas for service businesses.

Pet Pal: Give your neighbors an alternative to putting their pets in a kennel when they go out of town by feeding, walking, and playing with their pets.

Garden Guru: Hoe, weed, and make things grow!

Computer Consultant: Provide advice on navigating the World Wide Web. Teach a senior citizen how to send e-mail.

Binhex (BINary HEXadecimal) is a method for converting your non-text files (non-ASCII) into ASCII. This is necessary because Internet e-mail can only handle ASCII text.

Nice Neighbor: Look in on an elderly neighbor everyday, bring in the mail, take out the trash, sweep the steps or shovel the snow, and empty the kitty litter box.

Recycling Gopher: Offer to take bottles and cans to the redemption center for 50 percent of the refunded deposits. Bring neighbors' recyclables to the curb on recycling day.

Tutor: Teach younger kids to read or write, or help them with school subjects that are difficult for them. Teach them how to use the computer, play tennis, shoot baskets, or knit or sew. If you have a talent, you can always find a student!

Car Washer: Put on some old duds and use plenty of suds.

Lots of kids have made good money turning their talents or hobbies into businesses. Spencer Horsman, a professional ventriloquist, has been performing since he was 6 years old, when he first received a puppet as a gift. Way to go, Spencer!

Do you like to bake cookies? Can you tune up your own bike? Are you a whiz at figuring out how to use a new computer program?

Think of a potential business venture that seems both interesting and practical. Make a list of the start-up expenses for supplies, equipment, and fliers for your neighborhood.

Remember: The idea is to keep your costs as low as possible without compromising the quality of your service or product. So let's see what it takes to *estimate* costs and demand for your service or product before you spend a dime.

Let's say you're going to design one dozen T-shirts. How much will each shirt cost to make (called *cost of goods*)? To find out, check the cost for a package of plain T-shirts, and then divide to find out the cost for one shirt. Then calculate the cost of the other supplies you'll need, per shirt. What's your cost of goods?

COST OF GOODS

Supplies	Cost	Total Cost	Cost per Shirt (Total cost ÷ 12)
12 plain T-shirts	$6.99 for package of 3	$27.96	$2.33
fabric paints (3 colors, 2 bottles of each)	$1.49 per bottle	$8.94	$.75
		$42.10	$3.08

OVERHEAD

Costs of goods are one expense, but what about other expenses? These costs are called *overhead*. The interesting thing about overhead is that some of the costs stay the same whether you make one item or 12, so it is — you guessed it — better to make 12. Add all the overhead costs up and divide the total by 12 to find out how much your overhead will be for each shirt if you do 12 shirts as planned. Here are some overhead costs to think about:

- ◆ Will you be painting the shirts with paintbrushes, sponges, or silkscreening equipment? Call or visit a local craft store to find out how much these will cost.

- ◆ Will you be paying rent for the use of the garage where you plan to paint?

- ◆ What about advertising? Will you be printing fliers on your home computer or making them at a copy shop in town? (Don't forget to add the cost of the paper!)

COST OF OVERHEAD

Item	Total Cost
poster board and colored markers (for making display signs)	$7.50
book of sales receipts (to give customers)	$ .35
	$7.85

Add the overhead cost to the cost of goods. How much money will one shirt cost you to make now?

LABOR

Don't forget your time. How many hours does it take to complete one shirt? How about 12 shirts? Can you figure out your cost of labor per shirt?

To figure out what your time is worth (cost of labor), use the amount you get paid per hour mowing lawns or baby-sitting. That's what your time is worth at today's prices!

COST OF LABOR

hourly wage converted to wage per minute   x   estimated number of minutes per shirt

$4.50 per hour ÷ 60 minutes = 7$\frac{1}{2}$¢ per minute   x   30

Total Cost of Labor per shirt: $2.25

Total Cost of Labor: $27.00

COMPARATIVE PRICING

Now you can begin thinking about a selling price for your product. Once you've figured out the cost per shirt for supplies and overhead, research the price for similar products (in this case, decorated T-shirts) in your area. Let's say the average price is $10.00 a shirt, so that's the price you decide to set for your shirts as well. How much *revenue* (income) will you get at that price for 12 shirts? Now, subtract the cost of the goods and overhead. How many hours will you spend? Can you make any money at that price? Will it be worth the work?

revenue	(12 shirts x $10.00)	$120.00
minus what the shirts cost you	($42.10 for supplies + $7.85 for overhead)	–$49.95
minus your cost of labor to make 12 shirts		–$27.00
equals your profit		$43.05

Did you come out ahead of other jobs? (Divide your profit by the number of hours you spent working on your T-shirt business, including the time you spent advertising, buying supplies, decorating the shirts, and selling them. Then, you can compare what you made in your T-shirt business to what you make at other jobs.)

Other things to consider:

- Would you rather print T-shirts than mow lawns, even if you earned the same, or less?
- Can you afford the risk if your market "dries up"?
- Is your product good enough to enable you to raise the price $1.00 and still sell them?
- Is the demand steady? Could you sell 12 shirts a week for any length of time?

Make a Million!

Sometimes sticking with a job can pay off big. Really big. For fun, try striking a bargain with your parents in which you take on an extra chore, such as weeding the garden or setting the dinner table, for one month. Tell them you'll be happy with a starting pay of a nickel if they agree to double your salary every day for four weeks. Skeptical? Let's see who gets the better part of this deal!

1. Print the numbers 1 through 28 down the left-hand margin of a sheet of paper.

2. Print .05 next to number 1 to symbolize the nickel you'll earn for doing the chore on the first day.

3. Multiply your pay by 2 to find out how much you'll make on the second day, when your pay doubles. Write it on line 2.

4. Double your second day's wages to find out what you'll make on the third day. Write it on the line 3. Continue doubling each day's pay until all of the numbered lines are filled in with the correct figure.

5. Circle the date on which you can celebrate the end of your agreement. Now, for a real thrill, add up each day's wages to find your total earnings!

6. Can you believe your eyes? Yes, that's right, you earned a million dollars!

7. Consider letting your parents off the hook. After all, we all make mistakes from time to time. And remind them to always be careful what they agree to!

AN "INTEREST-ING" OPTION

In the old days, people used to hide their money — in the cookie jar, under a mattress, in the backyard — for safekeeping. These days, depositing your savings in a bank has a couple of advantages. (For one, you save room in the cookie jar for cookies!) And more to the point, your money will grow because banks pay *interest*. You see, the bank uses your money to loan to others; it doesn't just sit there waiting for you to take it back. In exchange for using your money, the bank pays you a percentage of your deposit. How can they afford to do that? Well, it's because they charge the people who borrow their money (actually *your* money) more than they pay you to use it, so they come out ahead!

There are two types of interest — *simple* and *compound*. Let's say you deposited $100 in a bank that offers 6 percent interest (that's .06 X $100 or 6¢ for every dollar you have in the bank). With *simple interest*, you will get paid $6 every year — the same amount of money every year on that initial deposit of $100.

With *compound interest*, the interest you earn each year will become part of your account if you leave it in the bank. This means that after you've earned $6 at the end of one year, you'll then begin to earn interest not only on that initial deposit of $100, but also on the $6 of interest the bank paid you. That way, *you can earn interest on your interest!* Over time, the difference between what you'll earn in simple interest versus compound interest becomes greater and greater.

	PIGGY BANK	SIMPLE INTEREST	COMPOUND INTEREST
TOTAL THE FIRST YEAR	— $100	$100 x .06 = $6 interest $106 in your account	$100 x .06 = $6 interest $106 in your account
TOTAL IN TWO YEARS	— $100	$100 x .06 = $6 interest $112 in your account	$106 x .06 = $6.36 interest $112.36 in your account
TOTAL IN THREE YEARS	— $100	$100 x .06 = $6 interest $118 in your account	$112.36 x .06 = $6.74 interest $119.10 in your account
TOTAL IN FOUR YEARS	— $100	$100 x .06 = $6 interest $124 in your account	$119.10 x .06 = $7.15 interest $126.25 in your account
TOTAL IN FIVE YEARS	— $100	$100 x .06 = $6 interest $130 in your account	$126.25 x .06 = $7.57 interest $133.82 in your account

P.S. If you added $100 of your own earnings to your account every year for five years, and then added 6 percent compounded interest, how much would you have after five years? (Find the answer on the next page.) See why savings pay off?

So what do you already know about savings?

1. Keeping your money in an interest-bearing account is much better than hiding it in a piggy bank at home.

2. Compound interest pays more over time than simple interest does.

3. The higher the interest rate that the bank pays, the better for you! So shop around!

Double Your Savings

Suppose you put $200 in a compound interest-earning savings account. How long would you have to leave it there to double your money? To find out, divide the interest rate into 72. (The number 72 is something Einstein, the mathematical genius, came up with, and it works every time!)

Say you're earning 6 percent interest.

72 ÷ 6 = 12

At the end of 12 years, your account balance would have doubled to $400. Wow!

How long would it take at 8 percent interest?

72 ÷ 8 = 9 years

Everything is relative, you know.

P.S.: You would have $597.53 ($500 of your own savings and $97.33 from the bank in interest).

INDEX

More Good Books from
WILLIAMSON PUBLISHING

Williamson books are available from your bookseller or directly from Williamson Publishing. Please see last page for ordering information or to visit our website. Thank you.

THE ORIGINAL WILLIAMSON'S *KIDS CAN!*® BOOKS ...

The following *Kids Can!*® books for ages 7 to 14 are each 144 to 176 pages, fully illustrated, trade paper, 11 x 8 ½, $12.95 US.

☆ American Bookseller Pick of the Lists
☆ 2000 American Institute of Physics Science Writing Award
☆ Parents' Choice Honor Award

GIZMOS & GADGETS
Creating Science Contraptions that Work (& Knowing Why)
BY JILL FRANKEL HAUSER

☆ American Bookseller Pick of the Lists
☆ Oppenheim Toy Portfolio Best Book Award
☆ Teachers' Choice Award

SUPER SCIENCE CONCOCTIONS
50 Mysterious Mixtures for Fabulous Fun
BY JILL FRANKEL HAUSER

☆ American Bookseller Pick of the Lists
☆ Parents' Choice Recommended

ADVENTURES IN ART
Arts & Crafts Experiences for 8- to 13-Year-Olds
BY SUSAN MILORD

☆ Parents Choice Silver Honor Award

THE KIDS' NATURAL HISTORY BOOK
Making Dinos, Fossils, Mammoths & More!
BY JUDY PRESS

☆ American Bookseller Pick of the Lists
☆ Oppenheim Toy Portfolio Best Book Award

THE KIDS' SCIENCE BOOK
Creative Experiences for Hands-On Fun
BY ROBERT HIRSCHFELD & NANCY WHITE

☆ Parents' Choice Gold Award
☆ Benjamin Franklin Best Juvenile Nonfiction Award

KIDS MAKE MUSIC!
Clapping & Tapping from Bach to Rock
BY AVERY HART AND PAUL MANTELL

☆ American Bookseller Pick of the Lists
☆ Dr. Toy Best Vacation Product

KIDS' CRAZY ART CONCOCTIONS
50 Mysterious Mixtures for Art & Craft Fun
BY JILL FRANKEL HAUSER

☆ Parents' Choice Recommended

KIDS' ART WORKS!
Creating with Color, Design, Texture & More
BY SANDI HENRY

JAZZY JEWELRY
Power Beads, Crystals, Chokers, & Illusion and Tattoo Styles
BY DIANE BAKER

☆ Selection of Book-of-the-Month; Scholastic Book Clubs

KIDS COOK!
Fabulous Food for the Whole Family
BY SARAH WILLIAMSON & ZACHARY WILLIAMSON

☆ Parents' Choice Recommended

THE KIDS' BOOK OF WEATHER FORECASTING
BY MARK BREEN AND KATHLEEN FRIESTAD

WILLIAMSON'S
KALEIDOSCOPE KIDS® BOOKS...
WHERE LEARNING MEETS LIFE

Kaleidoscope Kids® books for children, ages 7 to 14, explore a subject from many different angles, using many different skills. All books are 96 pages, two-color, fully illustrated, 10 x 10, $10.95 US.

☆ Parents' Choice Recommended
BRIDGES!
Amazing Structures to Design, Build & Test
BY CAROL A. JOHMANN AND ELIZABETH J. RIETH

☆ American Bookseller Pick of the Lists
☆ Children's Book Council Notable Book
☆ Dr. Toy 10 Best Educational Products
PYRAMIDS!
50 Hands-On Activities to Experience Ancient Egypt
BY AVERY HART & PAUL MANTELL

☆ American Bookseller Pick of the Lists
☆ Parent's Guide Children's Media Award
ANCIENT GREECE!
40 Hands-On Activities to Experience This Wondrous Age
BY AVERY HART & PAUL MANTELL

☆ American Bookseller Pick of the Lists
☆ Dr. Toy 100 Best Children's Products
☆ Parent's Guide Children's Media Award
KNIGHTS & CASTLES
50 Hands-On Activities to Experience the Middle Ages
BY AVERY HART & PAUL MANTELL

SKYSCRAPERS!
Super Structures to Design & Build
BY CAROL A. JOHMANN

GOING WEST!
Journey on a Wagon Train to Settle a Frontier Town
BY CAROL A. JOHMANN AND ELIZABETH J. RIETH

☆ American Bookseller Pick of the Lists
¡MEXICO!
40 Activities to Experience Mexico Past and Present
BY SUSAN MILORD

THE BEAST IN YOU!
Activities & Questions to Explore Evolution
BY MARC MCCUTCHEON

WHO *REALLY* DISCOVERED AMERICA?
Unraveling the Mystery & Solving the Puzzle
BY AVERY HART

☆ Teachers' Choice Award
GEOLOGY ROCKS!
50 Hands-On Activities to Explore the Earth
BY CINDY BLOBAUM

(PRICES MAY BE SLIGHTLY HIGHER WHEN PURCHASED IN CANADA.)